Celtic
First Names

George Mackay

**GEDDES &
GROSSET**

This edition published 1999 by Geddes & Grosset, an
imprint of Children's Leisure Products Limited

© 1999 Children's Leisure Products Limited, David Dale
House, New Lanark, ML11 9DJ, Scotland

ISBN 1 85534 951 5

Printed and bound in the UK

Introduction

LANGUAGES

The names in this book come from both strands of the Celtic language group: the *Goidelic* languages, Irish Gaelic, Scottish Gaelic, and Manx; and the *Brythonic* languages, Breton, Cornish and Welsh. Many of the older names are the same, or cognate (closely related) to each other in both language groups. There is a great deal of overlap between Scottish and Irish Gaelic usage; many names were brought into what was then Pictland by the Scots settlers, and for many hundreds of years after that there was in effect a unified cultural and linguistic

Gaelic-speaking community, crossed but not divided by political boundaries. This book attempts whenever possible to state on which side of the North Channel individual names, or forms of names, took shape. There are a number of Pictish names: the Picts spoke a form of Brythonic, though speculation continues as to whether they also spoke another language as well.

In addition it lists names whose origin is not Celtic but which have special significance in Celtic history and culture and which have often been given a Celtic form - Mary/Máire and David/Dafydd are examples; as well as names which have arisen in the Irish, Scots and Welsh forms of the English language.

PRONUNCIATION

A guide to pronunciation is given immediately after the details of language and gender, except for names where the pronunciation is obvious. Many of the names are from older forms of these languages, whose pronunciation was not necessarily the same as it is today. Pronunciation of any one language can also vary from one part of the country to another and the the pronunciation of a name sometimes also depends on the preference of the family naming the child. In the case of the few Pictish names included, pronunciation is a matter of linguistic speculation. As a result, this book can provide only an approximate guide to the pronunciation of the names.

A

Aamor *see* AENOR

Abán (Irish Gaelic, male) *Ab-ann*
'Little abbot', from *aba*, abbot. The anglicised form is Abban.

Adair (Irish Gaelic, male)
The root is Gaelic *doire*, 'oak wood', and the origin of the name may be 'dweller by the oak wood', or perhaps 'attendant of the oak grove', since the oak was a sacred tree in Celtic lore, tended by the druids.

Adamnan (Irish and Scottish Gaelic, male) *A-dawn-an*
Probably a pet form of Adam, little Adam. The

Gaelic form is both Adhamhán and Adomnán. St Adamnan, a seventh-century abbot of Iona, wrote his famous *Life of St Columba*.

Adeon (Welsh, male)
This name has been related to Welsh *adain*, 'wing', though perhaps it is a form of AEDDAN.

Aderyn (Welsh, female)
'Bird'. From *aderyn*, 'bird'.

Adhnúall (Irish Gaelic, male) *A-nooall*
'Sweet-sounding', from Gaelic *adnúall*, 'sweet of sound'. This was the name of one of the hounds of FIONN macCumhaill.

Adwen (Cornish, male)
'Fiery', a name related to Gaelic AED.

Aeb, Aebh *See* AOBH

Aebhric (Irish Gaelic, male) *Ive-rik*
This was the name of the monk of Erris who

wrote down the story of the *Children of Lír*.
English forms are Evric, Everett.

Aebill *see* AíBELL

Aed (Scottish and Irish Gaelic, male) *Aigh*
'Fiery one', from *áed*, 'fire'. A common name
among the Gaels, and said to have been the
most frequent personal name in early Ireland.
It was so common that most who had the
name had a further descriptive name or nickname, like Aed Finn (Gaelic *fionn*, 'fair') or
Aed Ruad (Gaelic *ruadh*, 'red'). It was the
name given to several high kings of Ireland
and a king of the Scots, son of Kenneth
MacAlpin. The name is also found as Aedh,
Aodh.

Aedh *see* AED

Aedammair (Irish Gaelic, female) *Ay-dammar*
A pet and feminine form of AED. Traditionally Aedammair was the first Irish nun.

Aedán (Scottish and Irish Gaelic, male) *Ay-dann*
A diminutive form of AED, with the -an suffix. The anglicised form is Aidan. An early king of Dalriada was named Aedán, as was the seventh-century Celtic missionary St Aidan, bishop of Lindisfarne, and twenty-two other saints of the Gaelic Church.

Aeddan (Welsh, male)
The name derives from *aed*, 'fire'. Aeddan was a warrior of the Old Welsh, featuring in the sixth-century poem 'Y Gododdin'.

Aedh *see* AED

Aednat (Irish Gaelic, female)
A diminutive form of AED. An alternative form is Aodhnait.

Ael (Breton, male) *Ale*
'Rocky', from *ail*, 'rock'. A name with a similar meaning to Peter.

Aelheran (Welsh, male) *Ale-eran*
'Iron-browed', from *ael*, 'brow', and *haearn*, 'iron'. A saint's name, preserved in Llanaelhaearn in Caernarfonshire.

Aelwen (Welsh, female)
'Fair-browed'.

Aelwyn (Welsh, male)
'Fair-browed', the masculine form of Aelwen.

Aengus *See* ANGUS

Aenor (Breton, Irish Gaelic, female) *Ay-nor*
From the Breton name Aamor, probably from a root-word meaning 'bright'.

Aerfen (Welsh, female)
'Renowned in battle'. This was the name of an early Welsh goddess, whose cult was linked to the River Dee in North Wales.

Aeron (Welsh, male)

The source of this name is unclear; some see it in Welsh *aeron*, 'berry'. But it is also the name of an early Welsh war-god, derived from the Brythonic Agroná, 'Slaughter'. Some scholars have identified it with the Scottish river name Ayr, but this has also been disputed.

Aeronwy (Welsh, female)

'The berry stream'. The name comes from the River Aeron in Ceredigion. Also found as Aeronwen.

Agnes (Scots, female)

Not Celtic by origin (from Greek *agneia*, 'pure'), this was a very popular name in Scotland until the late twentieth century. 'Black Agnes' Randolph, Countess of Dunbar, was a fourteenth-century heroine of the wars with the English. Pet forms include Aggie, Nancy.

Agroná *see* AERON

Aíbell (Irish Gaelic, female)
From Old Gaelic *áibel*, 'radiance', 'spark', this was the name of an old Irish goddess, later viewed as a fairy queen, with her mound at Craigeevil, near Killaloe in County Clare. She figures in numerous legends. Alternative forms of the name are Aebill, Aoibheall; anglicised to Aibinn or Eevin.

Aibgréne (Irish Gaelic, female) *A-grenya*
'Radiance of the sun', from Gaelic *grian*, 'sun'. The name of a daughter born to DEIRDRE and NAOISE, in the Legend of the Sons of Usna, who married the king of Tir nan Og.

Aibhlinn (Irish and Scottish Gaelic, female) *Ave-linn*
A form of Aveline (Norman French), anglicised into Evelyn.

Aibinn *see* AÍBELL

Aibreán (Irish Gaelic, female) *Ap-reeann*
'April'.

Aidan *SEE* AEDÁN

Aideen (Irish Gaelic, female)
A feminine form of AED. Aideen was the wife of the legendary warrior OSCAR, grandson of FIONN macCumhaill. *See also* ETAÍN.

Aife *SEE* AOIFE.

Aiken (Scots, male)
A pet form of Adam, shortened to Ad, with the diminutive suffix -kin added. Aiken Drum is the hero of a familiar Scottish nursery song.

Ailbe *see* AILBHE

Alaw (Welsh, female)
'Melodious'.

Ailbhe (Irish Gaelic, male/female) *Al-veh*
'White', from Old Gaelic *albho*, 'white'. Twelve warriors of the Fianna bore this name. Ailbe

16

is an alternative form; Ailbe Grùadbrecc, 'of the freckled cheeks', was wife to FIONN MacCumhaill after GRÁINNE.

Aileen (Scots, female)
An anglicised version of Gaelic EIBHLINN, Helen. *See* EILEEN. The form Aileen is also used on the Isle of Man.

Ailill (Irish Gaelic, male) *Al-yill*
A well-known name in ancient Ireland; the name of Queen MEDB's consort, and numerous other kings and heroes, probably derived from Gaelic *ail*, 'rock', though an alternative is 'sprite', as in Old Welsh *ellyll*. An anglicised version is Aleel.

Ailis (Irish Gaelic, female)
A Gaelic form of Alice.

Ailsa (Scots, female)
The name comes from Ailsa Craig, the rocky isle off the Ayrshire coast. Its derivation is

probably from the Old Norse proper name
AEL, with -ey, 'island'.

Aindrea (Scottish Gaelic, male)
A Gaelic form of ANDREW.

Aine (Irish Gaelic, female) *An-yeh*
'Brightness'. This was the name of an early
fertility goddess, who later was viewed as
a fairy queen. There are many legends
around her, including her bewitchment of
Maurice, Earl of Desmond, who however
gained control of her by seizing hold of her
cloak. Though often anglicised as Annie or
Anne, the names have quite separate
sources.

Aingeall (Irish and Scottish Gaelic, female) *An-gheeall*
'Angel'. *See also* Melangell.

Ainnle (Irish Gaelic, male) *Ann-leh*
One of the three sons of Usna, brother to

18

NAOISE, DEIRDRE's lover. Its derivation is unclear, but all three were famed warriors.

Ainslie (Scots, male/female)
A placename, from Old English *Aenes lie*, 'Aene's meadow', then a surname, and now increasingly used as a first name. Also found as Ainsley. Ainsley Gotto became famous in an Australian political scandal.

Aisling (Irish and Scottish Gaelic, female/male)
Ash-ling
From Gaelic *aisling*, 'dream', not used as a personal name until modern times. Other forms are Aislinn, Ashling.

Aislinn *see* AISLING

Alair (Irish Gaelic, male) *Allar*
'Cheerful', 'vital', from ALAIR, 'cheerful'.

Alan (Scottish Gaelic, male)
'Rock-like, steadfast'. From *ailinn* (Scottish

Gaelic) rock. *Ailean nan Sop*, 'Alan of the Straws' is a well-known character in Scottish Highland folk-tales. A popular name in Scotland since the time of the early Stewarts, when Alan FitzWalter, High Steward of Scotland, assumed the surname which was ultimately to be that of the royal line. In his case the name probably came from Brittany, though the root is the same. Other forms are Allan, Allen. *See* ALUN.

Alanna (Irish Gaelic, female)
From the Gaelic *a leanbh*, 'o child'.

Alasdair (Scottish Gaelic, male)
The Gaelic form of Alexander. This name was made popular by three kings, especially Alexander III (died 1293). Other forms are Alastair, Alister. Pet forms are Al, Aly. Aly Bain is a celebrated Shetland fiddle player.

Alastair *see* ALASDAIR

Alban (Scottish Gaelic, male)
'Scot'. The name comes from the Gaelic name for Scotland, Alba.

Alban (Welsh, male)
The name comes from St Alban, the Roman soldier who was the first British Christian martyr, in AD 303, and was venerated among the Brythonic tribes. The Latin name is Albanus, from *alba*, 'mountain'.

Alec, Alex, Alick (Scots, male)
Shortened forms of Alexander, sometimes used as names in their own right.

Aled (Welsh, male)
There is a river in Denbighshire of this name. Tudur Aled was a fifteenth-century poet, and more recently Aled Jones was a celebrated boy soprano singer. Another form is Aleid.

Aleel *see* AILILL

Aleid *see* Aled

Alexander (Scots, male)
Not a Celtic name in origin; an anglicised version of Greek *Iskander*, 'defender of men', made famous by Alexander the Great (*c.*360–330 BC). It became a very popular name in Scotland since three of the country's most effective medieval kings bore this name. *See* ALASDAIR.

Alice *see* AILIS, ALISON, ALYS, EILIS

Alison (Scots, female)
A Scots form of Alice, sometimes spelt Alyson or Alysoun. Alison Cockburn wrote a version of *The Flowers of the Forest*.

Alister *see* ALASDAIR

Allaid (Scottish Gaelic, male) *Allay*
A name from James Macpherson's Ossian poems of the eighteenth century, from Old Gaelic *allaid*, 'untamed', 'wild-living'.

Alma *see* ALMHA

Almha (Irish Gaelic, female) *Al-wah*
This was the name of a Celtic goddess associated with strength and healing. It has also picked up a connection with the non-Celtic name Alma, from Latin *alma*, 'dear'.

Alpin (Scottish Gaelic, male)
A Pictish name of uncertain derivation. Alpin was the father of Kenneth, first king of both the Pictish and Scottish nations.

Alva (Scots, female)
The name of a town in the Central district, from Gaelic *ail*, 'rock', *magh*, 'plain', but probably has also picked up associations with Alma (*see* ALMHA).

Alun (Welsh, male)
The Alun is a North Wales river name, whose origin means 'flowing among rocks' (similar to the Allan Water in Scotland). The personal name

may be from the river or may go back directly to the root-form *ail*, 'rock'. Alun of Dyfed figures in the *Mabinogion* tales. The name was taken as a bardic name by the nineteenth century Welsh bard John Blackwell. *See* ALAN.

Alwyn (Welsh, male)
From the River Alwen. Its derivation is from *ail*, 'rock', and *wyn*, 'white', a reminder of the Welsh song 'David of the White Rock'.

Alys (Welsh, female)
The Welsh form of Alice.

Alyson, Alysoun *see* ALISON

Amabel *see* MAB

Amalghaidh *see* AULAY

Amairgin (Irish Gaelic, male) *A-mar-yin*
'Wondrously born'. This name is borne by numerous figures in the early legends of Ireland.

Alternative forms include Amairgein, Amargen, and anglicised Amorgin.

Ambrose *see* EMRYS

Ambrosius (Latin, male) *see* EMRYS

Amlodd (Welsh, male) *Am-loth*
In Welsh Arthurian legend, Amlodd was the grandfather of King ARTHUR.

Ana *see* ANU

Anann *see* ANU

Anarawd (Welsh, male) *Ana-rodd*
'Most eloquent'. From *iawn*, 'most', 'highly', and huawdl, 'eloquent', as in modern Welsh *hwyl*.

Andrasta (Brythonic, female)
A goddess of the Celtic tribes in what is now England; the name means 'invincible'.

Andreas (Welsh, male)
The Welsh form of Andrew.

Andrew (Scots, male)
Although not a Celtic name, it early became a popular name for boys in Scotland because of the cult of the apostle St Andrew as the nation's patron saint. Many famous Scots have borne this name including the famous sailors Sir Andrew Barton and Sir Andrew Wood, and the philanthropic millionaire Andrew Carnegie. The form Andro is occasionally found; the pet forms are Andy, Andie.

Andrewina *see* ANDRINA

Andrina (Scots, female)
A female form of Andrew, popular when it was common for girls to be given a feminised version of their father's name. Another form is Andrewina.

Andro *see* ANDREW

Andy, Andie *see* ANDREW

Aneirin (Welsh, male) *An-eye-rin*
Perhaps a Welsh form of Latin *Honorius*, or
alternatively derived from the Welsh root
forms *an*, 'very', *eur*, 'golden', with the diminutive ending *-an*. Aneirin was one of the
earliest Welsh poets, author of 'Y Gododdin'.
The name is sometimes spelt Aneurin. Aneurin Bevan, Welsh Labour politician, introduced the British National Health Service in
the 1940s.

Aneurin *see* ANEIRIN

Angharad (Welsh, female) *Ang-harrad*
'The well-loved one'. In the seventh century
Angharad was the wife of RHODRI Mawr.

Angus (Scottish Gaelic, male)
'The unique one', or 'only choice'. The Gaelic
form is Aonghas, from a Pictish name
Oengus. A Pictish king of this name died in

AD 761, and his name is preserved in the former county of Angus. The form Oengus also figures in Old Irish literature, notably in the character of Angus Og, the god of youth.

Anluan (Irish Gaelic, male)
'Great hound', probably with the sense of great warrior.

Anne, Annie *see* AINE

Annwr (Welsh, female) *Ann-ur*
A feminine form of ANEIRIN. In the Arthurian legend, Annwr attempted to seduce ARTHUR.

Annwyl (Welsh, male) *Ann-ul*
'Very dear'.

Anwen (Welsh, female)
'Very fair'.

Anu (Irish Gaelic, female) *An-oo*
'Wealth', 'Abundance of riches'. The semi-

mythical Tuatha Dé Danann were 'the tribe of Anu'. She was a goddess of both good and evil, a figure of great power. Alternative forms are Ana, Anann. The name has no connection with 'Anne'.

Aobh (Irish Gaelic, female) *Ave*
'Radiant, attractive', from Old Gaelic *oíb*, 'attractiveness'. Aobh was the mother of the legendary *Children of Lir*, who were turned into swans. Other forms of the name are Aeb, Aebh.

Aoibheall *see* Aíbell

Aoibhín (Irish Gaelic, female) *Aiv-een*
'Shining one'. This was the name of numerous Irish princesses. *See also* Aoife, Eavan.

Aodh *See* Aed

Aodhagán (Irish Gaelic and Manx, male) *Ayd-a-gann*
'Little Aed'. The root is Gaelic *aed*, 'fiery'.

Aodhagán O Raithile was a notable lyric poet of the seventeenth century. The anglicised form is Egan.

Aodhnait *see* AIDNAIT

Aoife (Irish Gaelic, female) *Ay-fa*
An ancient name, stemming from Old Gaelic *aoibhinn*, 'of radiant beauty'. Nowadays it is often wrongly assumed to be a form of Eve, and often anglicised into Eva. Aoife was a Scottish 'Amazon' who bore a son to CUCHULAINN, whom the hero was later to unwittingly kill in battle. The name was borne by numerous other women of legend and history.

Aonghas *See* ANGUS

Archibald *See* GILLESPIE

Ardán (Irish Gaelic, male) *Ar-dann*
The third son of Usna, brother to *Naoise*, *Deirdre*'s lover. The derivation is from Old

Gaelic *ardàn*, 'pride'. In the tale he is referred to as 'fierce', or 'unyielding': it is certainly a warrior name.

Arddun (Welsh, female) *Arth-un*
'Beautiful one'.

Arduinna (Gaulish, female)
The name of a goddess of the Ardennes forest, whose symbolic animal was a boar. A hunting goddess, whose name has been linked with Greek Diana.

Argante (Old Gaelic, Welsh, male/female) *Arganta*
The name of a Celtic goddess of the underworld.

Arianrhod (Welsh, female)
'Silver disc'. This is the name of a goddess from the *Mabinogion* cycle of tales, associated with the Moon, beauty, inspiration and poetry.

Arlan (Cornish, male)
A legendary early saint of Cornwall, his name
perhaps a corruption of Allen or Elwin, also
Cornish saints.

Arlene (Gaulish, female)
Perhaps from the placename Arles.

Art (Irish Gaelic, male)
Probably from the same Indo-European root
as Greek *arctos*, 'bear'. The bear was celebrated for its strength. In Irish legend, the
best-known Art is a somewhat tragic hero, Art
Oenfer, 'the lonely', son of Conn of the Hundred Battles and father of Cormac macAirt.

Arthen (Welsh, male)
Cognate with Art, this was the name of a lo-
cal god in Wales, given also to a ninth-century king of Ceredigion.

Arthur (Welsh, male)
The name of the legendary leader of British

resistance to the invading Anglo-Saxons. The name has been linked to Greek *arctos*, 'bear', but also to a Celtic root form *ar*, 'plough', and to Brythonic *arddhu*, 'very black.' Its earliest appearance is in Welsh documents. The Gaelic form is Artair. In the North of Scotland, it may also be a form of the Old Norse name Ottar.

Asaf (Welsh, male) *Ass-af*
Name of the early Welsh saint who is commemorated in the North Wales bishopric of St Asaph.

Asaph *see* Asaf

Ash (English, male/female)
The ash tree, from Old English *aesc*, was widely worshipped among the Celtic peoples; ash, oak and thorn were a powerful triad. *See also* Rowan.

Ashling *See* Aisling

Atholl (Scottish Gaelic, male)
From the name of the Perthshire district, which comes from Gaelic *ath*, 'ford', and Fotla, name of one of the seven sons of the legendary founder of the Picts, CRUITHNE. Alternative forms are Athol, Athole.

Athracht (Irish Gaelic, female) *Ath-rach*
The name of a sixth-century Irish saint, from Gaelic *athrach*, 'change', perhaps describing the change of life from that of an aristocratic girl to that of a female hermit.

Aude (Cornish, female) *Awd-a*
In the French Chanson de Roland, Aude is a Breton princess betrothed to Roland. When Charlemagne wished instead to wed her to his son, she fell dead. The name also exists in Old Norse: Aud 'the Deep-Minded' was the founder of a colony on Iceland in the eleventh century.

Aulay (Scottish Gaelic, male)
The Gaelic form is Amalghaidh, a version of

Old Norse Olaf. The MacAulay clan claims a Viking origin.

Austell (Cornish, Breton, male) *Oss-tell*
A saint's name, of uncertain origin but perhaps linked with the placename Aust on the Bristol Channel. It is preserved in St Austell in Cornwall and Llanawastl in Wales.

Aveline *see* AIBHLINN

Awsten (Welsh, male) *Ow-sten*
Augustine in Welsh form. As the first archbishop of Canterbury, St Augustine had great prestige in Britain; it is he rather than St Augustine of Hippo who is commemorated.

B

Baibín (Irish Gaelic, female) *Ba-been*
A Gaelic form of Barbara. Báirbre is also
found. The popularity of the story of St
Barbara, killed by her father for refusing to
renounce Christianity, spread the name
through the Celtic world.

Báirbre *see* Baibín

Balor (Irish Gaelic, male)
Balor of the Evil Eye was a king of the
Fomorians, early invaders of Ireland, whose
baleful eye was never opened except on the
field of battle, where it rendered his enemies
powerless.

Banba (Irish Gaelic, female)
This very ancient name can also refer to the
land of Ireland itself; the original Banba came
to be seen as a tutelary goddess of Ireland.
Also found as Banbha. *See also* ERIN.

Banquo (Scottish Gaelic, male)
Familiar from Shakespeare's *Macbeth*, this
name of Macbeth's one-time comrade comes
from Gaelic *ban*, 'white', and *cú*, 'hound', suggesting a nickname origin.

Barbara *see* BAIBÍN

Barbe (Breton, female)
Name of a mythical saint who is neverthe-
less venerated in Brittany; probably as a
legacy from an earlier Celtic fire goddess, on
a similar mode to BRÍD.

Bard (All Celtic languages, male/female)
'Poet', 'singer'. This was an honoured profes-
sion in all Celtic communities. *See also* TADG.

Barr (Scottish Gaelic, male)
'Crest', 'top', perhaps signifying 'supreme'. St Barr is the same person as St Finbarr of Cork; his name is preserved in that of the island of Barra.

Barrfind (Irish Gaelic, male) *Barr-finn*
'Fair-haired', 'fair-crested'. The name is a turned-about form of FINBARR.

Barrie (Scots, male)
Also a surname, this name may come from a Norman immigrant who gave his name to Barry in Angus, but has also been traced back to Gaelic *bearrach*, 'spear'.

Beara (Irish Gaelic, female) *Bay-ara*
A legendary Irish princess.

Bearrach *see* BERRACH

Beathag *see* BETHÓC

Bébhionn *see* BÉBHINN

Bec (Irish Gaelic, female)
'Little one', from Gaelic *beag*, 'little'. Bec or Becca was a goddess of wisdom. But the name can also be a diminutive of non-Celtic Rebecca.

Becuma (Irish Gaelic, female)
The wife of CONN of the Hundred Battles. Becuma loved the king's son, ART, but married Conn for his power.

Bedivere *see* BEDWYR

Bedwyr (Welsh, male) *Bedd-uwir*
The name of the knight who was with King ARTHUR at his death, in the Round Table story. Its anglicised form is Bedivere.

Béibhinn (Irish Gaelic, female) *Bay-vin*
'Fair woman'. Related Gaelic forms are Béfind, Bébhionn. This name is found in numerous Gaelic love poems, and was also the name of the mother of king Brian Boruma. In

an anglicised form as Bevin or Bevan, it has been used as a boy's name. In the form Bhéibhinn, the first sound is 'v' and it has been confused with the unrelated Vivien/Vivian, a Norman-French name from Latin *vivere*, 'to live'.

Bel *see* BELENNUS

Belenos *see* BELENUS

Belenus (Gaulish, male)
Perhaps from a Celtic root word meaning 'bright', this was the name of one of the chief gods of the pre-Christian Celts. It is found in other forms such as Bel, Belenos, Belus.

Bella (Scots, female)
Though not of Celtic derivation, the use of the suffix of Isabella and similar names as a name in its own right is distinctively Scots.

Belus *see* BELENUS

Befind *see* BEBHINN

Berchan (Scottish Gaelic, male)
Name of a tenth-century holy man who compiled a 'Prophecy' or history of the kingdom of the Picts and Scots.

Beriana *see* BURYAN

Berrach (Irish Gaelic, female)
The source of the name is uncertain, but Berrach Breac, 'the freckled', third wife of FIONN macCumhaill, was said to be the most generous woman in Ireland. An alternative form is Bearrach.

Berwyn (Cornish, Welsh, male)
Berwyn was an early Celtic saint whose name is preserved in the Berwyn Ranges of mountains in North Wales and in Merioneth.

Betrys (Welsh, female)
The Welsh form of 'Beatrice'.

Bethan, Beatha (Irish Gaelic, female) *Bay-han*, *Bay-ha*
Probably from Gaelic *beatha*, 'life'. In old Scotland this was also a male name: Macbeth, eleventh-century king of Scots, means literally 'son of life'.

Bethan (Welsh, female)
A diminutive form of 'Elizabeth', but often used as a name in its own right.

Bethóc (Scottish Gaelic) *Bay-ock*
This was the daughter of SOMERLED, Lord of Argyll. Also written Beathag. Related to Bethan, it is Gaelic *beatha*, 'life'.

Beuno (Welsh, male) *By-no*
A seventh-century Welsh saint, whose name is preserved in St Beuno's Well, subject of a poem by Gerald Manley Hopkins.

Beynon (Welsh, male)
'Son of EINION'.

Biddy, Biddie *see* BRÍD

Bile (Irish Gaelic, Pictish) *Bee-la*
'Noble warrior'. In Irish legend Bile was a leader of the Milesians, one of the early invading groups. In Scotland he was the father of the Pictish king Bridei, whom St Columba visited.

Bladud (Brythonic, male)
A mythical king from old British tales; allegedly founder of the city of Bath and father of King Lear.

Bláithin (Irish Gaelic, female) *Bla-hin*
'Flower', 'blossom', from *bláth*, 'flower'. Other names of the same meaning are Blathnáid and Bláthnaid. *See also* BLODWEN.

Blair (Scottish Gaelic, male)
A surname and location name but quite often used as a first name, from Gaelic *blár*, 'field', 'battleground'.

Blaise (Breton, Cornish, male)
The name may derive from Breton *blas*, 'taste'.
It is preserved in St Blazey in Cornwall, and
in France was the name of the religious phi-
losopher Blaise Pascal. An alternative form
is Bleise, in Celtic legend the tutor of the ma-
gician MYRDDYN, 'Merlin'.

Bláithín *see* BLÁTHNAT

Blánaid *see* BLÁTHNAT

Blane (Irish and Scottish Gaelic, male)
From St Bláan, whose name is preserved in Scottish towns such as Dunblane and Blanefield

Blathnáid, Bláthnaid *see* BLÁITHIN

Bláthnat (Irish Gaelic, female) *Bla-na*
'Little flower'. Related Gaelic forms are
Blánaid, Bláithín. Bláthín, wife of the chief-
tain Cú Roí, betrayed him to his enemy
CUCHULAINN and was killed by Ferchertne, his

faithful bard, who clasped her to him and leapt from a cliff-top.

Bleddyn (Welsh, male) *Bleth-in*
'Wolf-like', from *blaidd*, 'wolf'. Bleddyn ap Cynfryn was a prince in the eleventh century.

Bleise *see* BLAISE

Blodeuedd (Welsh, female) *Blod-wedd*
'Flower face'. A beautiful woman created by the mages GWYDION and Math to be wife to the hero Lleu Llaw Gyffes, but who betrays him and is ultimately turned into an owl; the story is in the Mabonogion cycle.

Blodwen (Welsh, female)
'White flower', from *blodau*, 'flowers'; *ven*, 'white'.

Bonnie (Scots, female)
The Scots adjective *bonnie*, 'beautiful',

reimported from North America as a first name. In the USA it was made famous or notorious by the girl gangster Bonnie Parker.

Bran (Common to all Celtic languages, male) 'Raven', or 'crow', the name of a god who was believed to possess powers of life and death. The name occurs in legends of all the Celtic countries.

Brandubh (Irish and Scottish Gaelic) *Bran-doov* 'Black raven'. A name borne by a number of provincial kings. An anglicised form is Branduff.

Brangaine (Irish Gaelic, female) *Bran-gy-ana* A Gaelic form of Bronwen. Brangaine was the nurse of ISEULT who gave her and TRYSTAN a love potion.

Branwen *see* BRONWEN

Bregeen (Irish, female) *Bregh-een*
'Little Bridget'. *See* Bríd.

Brenda (Scots, female)
Often taken as Celtic but it is not a feminine version of Brandon. It is more likely to be from an Old Norse source, *brandr*, 'sword'.

Brendon (Irish and Scottish Gaelic, male)
Perhaps derived originally from the Old Gaelic *bran*, 'raven', though a link with Welsh *brenhyn*, 'prince', has also been proposed. This was the name of the energetic and far-travelled saint Brendan of Clonfert, 'Brendan the Navigator' (died AD 577), who, according to some, traversed the Atlantic in his coracle. An alternative form is Brandon.

Brett (Breton, male)
'Briton', from Breizh, the Breton name of Brittany. Sometimes found as Bret, as in the name of the comic poet Bret Harte.

Brian (Irish Gaelic, male) *Breye–an.* (The Gaelic pronunciation is *Bree-an*)

Possibly Breton in origin, from a root-word *bri*, 'dignity, pride'. It gained great prestige from Brian Boruma, 'of the cattle taxes', high king of Ireland (*c.* 941–1014) victor and victim of the Battle of Clontarf, at which Viking rule in Ireland was broken, and progenitor of the O'Briens. The form Brion is also found and the form Bryan is also a common spelling.

Briana (Irish) *Bree-ana*
Feminine form of Brian.

Brice (Welsh, male)
From *ap-Rhys*, 'son of Rhys', ('the burning or ardent one'). An alternative form is Bryce.

Bríd (Irish Gaelic, female) *Breeth*
A name of power in the old Celtic world, belonging to a goddess whose name is associated with Gaelic *brígh*, 'power, virtue'. As-

similated into the Christian tradition, the goddess became a venerated saint; indeed there are sixteen or more Saint Bridgets, of whom the fifth-century St Bridget of Kildare is the best-known; and the name was carried to Scotland in the sixth century as St Bride. The name has numerous forms: Bridget, Brigid, Brigit, are the most frequent, with pet forms Biddy, Biddie (Ireland) and Bridie (Scotland). The Breton name Berc'hed is another form. For centuries it was the most popular girl's name in Ireland, as synonymous with an Irish girl as Patrick was with a boy.

Bride, Bridget, Brídie, Brigid, Brigit *see* Bríd

Bridei *see* Brude

Brieuc *see* Brioc

Brioc (Welsh, male)
St Brioc (sixth century) is also known in Brittany as St Brieuc.

Brion *see* BRIAN

Brisen (Welsh, female) *Bree-sen*
The name of a witch from the Arthurian legends.

Brix *see* BRUCE

Brochfael (Welsh, male) *Broch-file*
A legendary king, mentioned in the songs of the minstrel TALIESIN.

Brógán (Irish Gaelic, male) *Broh-gawn.*
Of uncertain derivation, this was the name of a number of early holy men, including St Brógán who acted as a scribe for St Patrick.

Brona, Bronach *see* BRÓNAGH

Brónagh (Irish Gaelic, female) *Broh-na*
'Sorrowing', from Gaelic *brónach*, 'sorrowful.' A Celtic equivalent of the name Dolores. Indeed, some Irish girls have been called Do-

lours, perhaps by parents unaware of the availability of Brónagh. Also found as Brona, Bronach.

Brongwyn *see* Bronwen

Bronwen (Welsh, female)
'White-breast'. *Bron*, 'breast'; *ven*, 'white'. Other forms are Brongwyn, Branwen. *See also* Brangaine.

Bruce (Scots, male)
Originally a surname, from Norman-French Brix, a location in Normandy. This became de Brus, then Bruce, the family name of king Robert I of Scotland. It became a popular first name from the nineteenth century, especially in Australia.

Brude (Pictish, male)
Bruide or Bridei, anglicised to Brude, was the king of the Picts whom St Columba visted in AD 565.

Bruide *see* BRUDE

Bryan *see* BRIAN

Brychan (Welsh, male) Bree-chan
'Freckled one'. A fifth-century chief whose name is preserved in Brecon and Castell Brychan, Aberystwyth.

Bryce (Welsh, male) *See* BRICE

Bryn (Welsh, male) Brinn
'Hill'. Not connected with Brian.

Brynmawr *see* BRYNMOR

Brynmor (Welsh, male)
'Great hill'. *Bryn*, 'hill'; *mor*, 'great'. Also spelt as Brynmawr.

Buan (Irish Gaelic, male/female) *Bwan*
'Lasting', 'enduring'.

Budoc (Cornish, male)
The patron saint of Cornwall; his name preserved in St Budeaux. The name has the same form as Boudicca, and is probably from the same root, *buad*, 'victory'. The Welsh name Buddug is cognate with Budoc.

Buddug *see* BUDOC

Buryan (Cornish, female)
'Gift', probably related to Gaelic *beir*, 'gift'. Buryan or Beriana was a Cornish saint. The name Veryan is probably from the same source.

C

Cabhán (Irish Gaelic, male) *Ca-vann*
The name of an Irish county, derived from
Gaelic *cabhán*, 'grassy hill', or 'grassy hollow',
referring to a hilly countryside. A name similar in sound to Caoimhín, KEVIN, but unrelated.

Cadan (Irish Gaelic, male) *Cad-an*
'Wild goose', the name of a mythical hero of
early legend.

Cadell (Welsh, male)
A warrior's name, from *cad*, battle.

Cadfael (Welsh, male) *Cad-file*
'Battle prince'. The name has been made famous
by the Brother Cadfael stories by Ellis Peters.

Cadoc *see* CADOG

Cadog (Welsh, male)
A warrior name, from *cad*, 'battle'. But the most famous Cadog was a saint of the sixth century, whose name is preserved in places such as Llangattock. It is also found as Cadoc.

Cadwallader *see* CADWALADR

Cadwaladr (Welsh, male)
'Leader in battle', from *cad*, 'battle'; *gwaladr*, 'leader'. The name of legendary heroes, and of the sixth-century prince of Gwynedd, Cadwaladr Fendigaid, 'blessed', who died in Rome in the later seventh century. It is also found using the anglicised spelling as Cadwallader.

Cadwallon (Welsh, male)
From Welsh *cad*, 'battle', and *gallon*, 'scatterer', 'ruler'.

Cadwgan (Welsh, male) *Cad-o-gan*
Another name deriving from *cad*, 'battle'.
Cadwgan is a tenth-century Welsh chieftain
associated with Glamorgan, where there is a
hill called Moel Cadwgan. The anglicised
form is Cadogan.

Cáel (Irish Gaelic, male) *Kyle*
'Slender one'. A hero of the Fianna, lover of
Créd.

Cáelfind (Irish Gaelic, female) *Kyle-finn*
'Slender and fair', from *caol*, 'slender' and *fionn*,
'fair'. An alternative Gaelic form is Caoilainn.
This name was born by a number of holy
women. The anglicised form is Keelin or Ceelin.

Caerwyn (Welsh, male) *Carr-win*
'White fort'.

Cahir *see* CATHAÍR

Cai *see* CEI

Cailean *see* Colin

Caindce *see* Cainche

Cainche (Irish Gaelic) *Cann-hya*
'Melody', 'songbird'. A daughter of Fionn macCumhaill, who bears a son to Fionn's enemy Goll macMorna. An alternative form is Caince.

Cairbre (Irish Gaelic, male) *Carr-bra*
The name probably means 'charioteer'; the great warriors had their personal charioteers, who were not themselves fighting men. A frequent name in Old Irish sources. It is applied to a high king, Cairbre Lifechair, 'of the Liffey', in the tales of the Fenian Cycle.

Cairean *see* Cairenn

Cairenn (Irish Gaelic, female) *Carr-enn*
Perhaps taken into the Celtic languages from Latin *carina*, 'dear'. The name of the mother

of the early Irish high king NIALL of the Nine
Hostages, founder of the Ui Neills. She was
not the wife of Niall's father but a concubine,
traditionally a slave from Britain. An alternative Gaelic version is Caireann, and it is
sometimes anglicised to Carina and Karen.

Cáit (Irish Gaelic, female) *Kawt*
A shortened form of Caitlín.

Caitlín (Irish Gaelic, female) *Kawt-leen*
A Gaelic form of Norman-French Cateline, a
form of Catherine. The anglicised version is
Cathleen or Kathleen.

Calder (Scots Gaelic, female)
From a Gaelic compound meaning 'stream by
the hazels', a location name from several parts
of Scotland that has become a surname and
an occasional first name.

Calgacus (Latin, male)
The name given by Tacitus to the the com-

mander of the Caledonian tribes at the battle of Mons Graupius, AD 83. Said to mean 'sword wielder', it is the oldest recorded name of an inhabitant of what is now Scotland.

Callum (Scottish Gaelic, male)
Scottish Gaelic form of Latin *columba*, 'dove'. Also found as Calum. *See* MALCOLM.

Calum *see* CALLUM

Cameron (Scottish Gaelic, male/female)
A surname, from Gaelic *cam*, 'hooked, bent' and *sron*, 'nose'. Originally probably only given to boys whose mothers' maiden name was Cameron, but now in general use and increasingly given to girls as well.

Campbell (Scottish Gaelic, male) *Cam-bell*
A surname, from Gaelic *cam*, 'bent, wry', and *beul*, 'mouth', so originally a nickname. Its use as a first name probably began in the same way as Cameron.

Canice (Irish, male)
An anglicised form of Gaelic *Coinneach*,
Kenneth. Kilkenny Cathedral is dedicated to
St Canice, and shows the same name in a dif-
ferent form: *cill*, 'church', Coinneaich, 'of
Kenneth'. *See also* KENNETH.

Caoilainn *see* CÁELFIND

Caoilfhinn (Irish Gaelic, female) *Kyle-finn*
'Slender fair one'. *Caol*, 'slender', *fionn*, 'fair'.
Other forms of the same name are Kaylin,
Keelan. *See also* CÁELFIND.

Caoimhe *see* KEVA

Caoimhín *see* Kevin

Caomh (Irish Gaelic, male) *Kave*
From Gaelic *caomh*, 'gentle', 'noble'. A leg-
endary warrior, and progenitor of the
O'Keeffes.

Cara (Irish Gaelic, female)
'Friend'. *See also* CERA.

Caractacus *see* CARADOG

Caradoc *see* CARADOG

Caradog (Welsh, male)
An early Welsh chieftain who fought against
the Romans in the first century AD. They rendered the name as 'Caractacus'. The Irish
form is Cárthach, and an anglicised form is
Caradoc. Caer Caradoc (Caradoc's fort) is a
hill in Shropshire.

Carey (Brythonic, female)
The place and river name Cary occurs in Som-
erset, England, and in central Scotland, and may
be from the Celtic root car, 'dark', which is also
the source of Kerry in Ireland. An association
may also have grown up with Latin *cara*, 'dear'.
The phrase 'Mother Carey's chickens' is from
Latin *mata cara*, meaning the Virgin Mary.

Cariad (Welsh, female)
'Loved one'.

Carina *see* CAIRENN

Carl *see* CERBHALL

Caron (Welsh, male) *Carr-on*
The name of a saint, found in the placename
Tregaron, in Ceredigion.

Caronwyn (Welsh, female)
'Beautiful loved one', from *caru*, 'to love', and
gwyn, 'white, fair'.

Carroll *See* CERBHALL

Cárthach *see* CARADOG

Cartimandua (Latinised Brythonic, female)
The nameof the first-century AD queen of
the Brigantes, in what is now northern England.

Carwen (Welsh, female) *Carr-wen*
'White love', from *caru*, 'to love' and *ven*, 'white'.

Carwyn (Welsh, male)
The male form of Carwen.

Cary (Brythonic, male)
A masculine form of Carey.

Caryl (Welsh, female)
Another name deriving from *caru*, 'to love'.

Carys (Welsh, female)
'Loved', from *caru*, 'to love'.

Casey (Irish Gaelic, male)
'Vigilant in war', from Irish Gaelic *cathasach*, 'battle-alert'. A surname that is seeing more use as a first name.

Cassivellaunus (Latin, male)
Latinised form of a Celtic name, that of a first-

century tribal king of Southern Britain who fought against Julius Caesar's invading troops.

Caswallon (Welsh, male)
This hero of the *Mabinogion* tales who conquers Britain may be modelled at least in part on CASSIVELLAUNUS.

Catháir (Irish Gaelic, male) *Ka-har*
Probably derived from cath, 'battle', and meaning 'battle-lord'. The anglicised form is Cahir.

Cathal (Irish Gaelic, male) *Ka-hal*
'Strong battler', from *cath*, 'battle'. Cathal Brugha (1874–1922) was a leader of the 1916 Easter Rising, and was killed in the Irish Civil War in 1922.

Cathán (Irish Gaelic, male) *Ka-hann*
'Warrior', from *cath*, 'battle'. The name of a descendant of NIALL of the Nine Hostages, who was the founder of the O' Kanes.

Cathbad (Irish Gaelic, male) *Cath-bat*
Incorporating the stem *cath*, 'battle', this was the name of a celebrated druid, who warned the men of Ulster of the baneful future awaiting the baby DEIRDRE. It has been anglicised to Cuthbert.

Cathella (Scots, Irish, female)
A combination of parts of Catherine and Isabella: not Celtic in origin but very much a Scottish and Irish name.

Catherine *see* CATRIONA, CATRIN, KAY

Cathleen *See* CAITLÍN

Catrin (Welsh, female)
The Welsh form of Catherine.

Catriona (Scottish and Irish Gaelic, female)
The Gaelic form of Catherine. The fourth-century martyr St Catherine of Alexandria achieved international renown, and St

Catherine of Siena (1347–1380) added further lustre to the name. In more modern times, Robert Louis Stevenson's novel *Catriona*, the sequel to *Kidnapped*, also popularised the name. A pet form of this name is Trina.

Ceallach (Irish Gaelic, male/female)
'Bright-headed'. Ceallach Cualand was the father of St KENTIGERN, or MUNGO, of Glasgow. An alternative form is Cellach, and the anglicised form is Kelly.

Ceara *see* CERA

Cecil (Welsh, male)
Stemming from Welsh *seisyllt*, 'sixth', which could mean sixth child, like Latin Sextus. But its use as a first name seems to come from the fame of the surname Cecil in England, where it is the family name of the marquesses of Salisbury.

Ceelin *see* CÁELFIND

Cei (Welsh, male) *Kay*
Possibly from the common Latin name Caius, which would have been frequently found in Roman Britain. In Welsh legend, a companion to King ARTHUR and steward of his household. It is also found as Cai. His name has been anglicised to Sir KAY in the English Arthurian tales.

Ceinwen (Welsh, female) *Kyne-wen*
'Fine white one', from *cein*, 'elegant', 'fine'; *ven*, white. Her name is preserved in St Keyne's Well, near Liskeard.

Ceiriog (Welsh, male) *Kye-riog*
A river name from North Wales.

Cellach *see* CEALLACH

Cennydd (Welsh, male) *Kennith*
The Welsh saint Cennydd, whose name, cognate with Irish CINÁED, is preserved in Senghennydd in Glamorgan.

Cera (Irish Gaelic, female) *Kee-ra*
This name goes a long way back in Irish legend to the wife of Nemed, leader of the Nemedians, the third set of invaders of ancient Ireland. It was also borne by three saints. An alternative form is Ceara. It is liable to be confused with CARA.

Cerbhall (Irish Gaelic, male) *Kerr-wal.*
'Brave in battle'. A name borne by several kings in the Gaelic period, and by the fifth President of the Irish Republic, Cearbhall O Dálaigh. Anglicised forms include Carroll and Carl, though in this latter form it is likely to be confused with German Carl or Karl.

Ceredig (Welsh, male)
'Lovable', 'kind one'. Ceredig was a sixth-century king of the Strathclyde Britons. Ceredigion in Wales is called after another Ceredig, son of the semi-legendary fifth-century king Cynedda. The anglicised form is Cardigan.

Ceri (Cornish, Welsh, male/female) *Kerri*
'Loved' from *caru*, 'to love'. Ceri Richards (1903–1977) was a distinguished twentieth-century artist

Ceridwen (Welsh, female) *Ker-idwen*
The Welsh poetic muse, mother of the minstrel Taliesin. From *cerdd*, 'poetry', and *ven*, 'white'.

Cernunnos (Gaulish, male) *Ker-nunnos*
'Horned one'. An important god of the continental Celts, portrayed with the body of a man and the head of a stag.

Cethern (Irish Gaelic, male) *Ke-hern*
'Long-lived'. Cethren is an alternative form of the name.

Chrissie (Scots, Irish, male/female)
In Scotland, a typical pet form of Christine, but in Ireland often a pet form of the boy-name Christopher.

Ciabhán (Irish Gaelic, male) *Keea-vann*
'Full-haired'. Ciabhán 'of the flowing locks'
was the lover of Clídna, with whom he eloped
from the land of the sea-god, Manannan. The
anglicised form is Keevan.

Ciara (Irish and Scottish Gaelic) *Kee-ara*
'Dark one', from *ciar*, 'dark'. Anglicised forms
of the name include Keera, Keira, Kira.

Ciarán (Irish and Scottish Gaelic, male) *Kee-rann*
'Little dark one', from *ciar*, 'dark', with the
diminutive suffix *-an*. Among several saints
to bear the name, perhaps the most celebrated is the founder of the abbey of
Clonmacnoise in AD 547, the year of his
death. Anglicised forms include Kieran. *See
also* KERR.

Cináed (Pictish) *Kin-aith*
A name borne by kings of the Northern Irish
Picts. It has been linked to Gaelic Coinneach,
KENNETH, but this link is uncertain.

Cledwyn (Welsh, male)
This is a Denbigh river name, though a derivation from Welsh cledd, 'sword', is perhaps more likely for the personal name. Cledwyn Hughes, later Lord Cledwyn was a prominent political figure in the 1960s and 70s.

Clídna *see* CLÍODHNA

Clíodhna (Irish Gaelic, female) *Klee-ona*
The derivation is unclear. In legend she was one of the three daughters of a prince of the sea kingdom of Mannannan, who eloped with CIABHÁN, son of the king of Ulster, and was drowned in punishment by a tidal wave. An alternative form is Clídna, and the anglicised form is Cliona.

Clíona *see* CLÍODHNA

Clodagh (Irish Gaelic, female) *Kloda*
Probably from the river name Clóideach, in County Tipperary.

Clyde (Scots, male)
The Scottish river name was taken up outside Scotland as a first name, especially in the USA, and was reimported to Scotland. In America its most notorious holder was the gangster Clyde Barrow, shot dead in 1934.

Coel (Welsh, male) *Koil*
'Trust'. Coel was a king in the British kingdom of Strathclyde; in fact probably the origin of 'Old King Cole'.

Coinneach *see* KENNETH

Col *see* COLIN

Colla (Irish Gaelic, male)
'Lord'. A frequent name in early Irish legend. The Clan Donald traces its origins back to Colla Uais, an Irish prince of the fifth century.

Colleen (Irish Gaelic, female)
'Girl', from Gaelic *cailin*, 'girl', 'maiden'. The

generic word for a girl has been taken up as an individual name.

Colin (Scottish Gaelic, male)

The Gaelic form is Cailean, 'youth', and it has close associations with the Campbell clan, whose chief has the Gaelic title MacCailein Mór, 'son of Great Colin'. Unrelated to this is the Irish Cóilín, formed from Col, an abbreviation of 'Nicholas', as is the English name 'Colin'.

Colm (Irish Gaelic, male) *Collum*

'Dove'. The derivation from is Latin *columba*, 'dove'. The most famous bearer of the name is Columcille, 'dove of the church', the Gaelic name of St Columba, founder of Irish monasteries at Durrow, Kells, and other places, and who, when expelled from Ireland for pride and contumacity, established himself on Iona, where he died in 597, having become the most celebrated missionary saint of Scotland. *See* CALUM.

Colmán (Irish Gaelic, male) *Collaman*
'Little dove'. Many holy men bore this name in Ireland and in Scotland, and it is preserved in many place names.

Columbanus (Latin, male)
'Little dove'. A Latinised form of Colmán. St Columbanus (died AD 615) was one of the missionaries who brought Christianity to central Europe; his hermitage-cave near Interlaken in Switzerland can still be visited.

Comgall (Irish Gaelic, male) *Cow-al*
St Comgall founded the monastery at Bangor, County Down. Cowal in Scotland is named after Comhghall, a descendant of the first Dalriadic kings. An alternative form is Comghall.

Comghall, Comhghall *see* COMGALL

Conaire (Irish Gaelic, male) *Con-yara*
A legendary hero and high king of Ireland. The root of the name is *cú*, 'hound'.

Conall (Irish Gaelic, male)
'Wolfish', from Gaelic *cú,* which means 'wolf' as well as 'hound'. Conall Cearnach, 'victorious', is one of the heroes of the *Ulster Cycle* of legends. The anglicised form is Connel, or Connell.

Conan (Welsh, male)
Perhaps from a verb meaning 'to grumble'.

Conán (Irish Gaelic, male) *Con-ann*
From Gaelic *cú,* 'hound', 'wolf'. In the Fenian Cycle of legends Conán macMorna, one of the Fianna, plays the part of a mischief-maker and boaster.

Conachar *see* CONCHOBAR

Conchobar (Irish Gaelic, male) *Con-ko-warr*
The name means 'lover of hounds', and was borne most famously by Conchobar macNessa, king of Ulster and frustrated lover of Deirdre. There are many other stories in

which he appears. The name has a variety of forms, including Conchubor, Conchobhar, Conachar, and the anglicised Conor or Connor.

Conchobhar, Conchubor *see* Conchobar

Conn (Irish Gaelic, male)
The source of the name is variously taken as from *cú*, 'hound', 'wolf'; or from an Old Gaelic root word implying wisdom. The name is borne by some celebrated figures of antiquity, including Conn Céadcathach, 'of the hundred battles', high king of Ireland and regarded as the progenitor of several noble families in Ireland and Scotland.

Connel, Connell *see* Conall

Connla (Irish Gaelic, male)
'Little hound'. The name of the son of Cuchulainn and Aoife, slain in fight by Cuchulainn who did not know who he was.

Connor, Conor *see* CONCHOBAR

Conwy (Welsh, male) *Konn-wee*
A river name originally, also later that of a famous castle, used as a first name in modern times. The anglicised form is Conway.

Cormac (Irish Gaelic, male) *Corra-mac*
Probably from Gaelic *corb*, 'chariot', with *mac*, 'son'. A popular name in the Gaelic world. Cormac macAirt is the first high king of Ireland recorded as having his capital at Tara (third century AD). The hero of many stories, he left a reputation for wisdom and prudence. The anglicised form is Cormack.

Cormack *see* CORMAC

Cospatrick (Welsh/Gaelic, male)
'Servant of Patrick'. This name is an anglicised version of *gwas* (Old Welsh) 'servant', and PADRUIG.

Craig (Scottish Gaelic, male)
'Rock', from *carraig*, 'rock, crag'.

Créd (Irish Gaelic, female) *Craith*
The name of a daughter of the king of Kerry,
wooed and won by CÁEL. After his death in
the battle of Ventry, she commits suicide.

Creidne (Irish Gaelic, female) *Craith-nya*
'Loyal'. In Irish legend Creidne was a female
member of the Fianna, the troop of warrior-
bards who were bodyguards to various kings
and high kings. In Celtic legend, female warriors were by no means unusual.

Creiddlad, Creiddylad *see* CREUDDYLAD

Creuddylad (Welsh, female) *Kry-the-lad*
The Welsh form of Cordelia. In the story of
Culhwych ac Olwen, a maiden of this name is
described as the most majestic who ever
lived. Other forms are Creiddylad,
Crieddlad.

Criomhthann *see* CRIMTHANN

Crimthann (Irish Gaelic, male) *Creev-thann*
'Fox', implying cleverness. An alternative
form is Criomhthann. This was a name given
to Colum Cille before he entered the church.

Crisiant (Welsh, female) *Krees-yant*
Derived from *crisial* meaning 'crystal'.

Cruithne (Old Gaelic, male) *Kroo-eena*
This was the Gaelic name given to the founder
of the Picts, whose seven sons represent the
seven provinces of Pictland. It was also used as
a female name, as in Cruithne, the daughter of
the great smith and weapon-maker Lóchan.

Crystyn (Welsh, female)
'Follower of Christ', the Welsh form of
'Christina'.

Cuchulainn (Irish Gaelic, male) *Koo-hoolin*
'Hound of Culann'. When the boy Setanta

killed Culann's hound, he promised to play
the part of the dog himself, and took this
name accordingly: one of many evidences in
Celtic lore of shape-changing between people and animals. The boy went on to become
the great hero of the *Ulster Cycle* of legends.

Cuilean (Scottish Gaelic, male) *Cul-yan*
From *cúilean*, 'whelp'; the name of a tenth-cen-
tury contender for the kingship of the Picts and
Scots, killed in battle against King Indulf.

Culann (Irish Gaelic, male)
Known from the Cuchulainn story, this name
of a legendary smith, maker of the armour of
Conchobhar macNessa, king of Ulster, is probably formed from the Old Gaelic root word *col*,
'chief'. Its anglicised form is Callan or Cullen.

Culhwych (Welsh, male) *Kool-hooh*
The name may stem from an Old Welsh root-
word meaning 'pig-lord'. It was borne by the
hero of the old Welsh legend of *Culhwych ac*

Olwen. Culhwych, son of Cilydd, bears a curse from before his birth which can only be ended when he wins the love of OLWEN, daughter of the giant Ysbaddaden.

Cunobelinus (Latin, male)
Latinised form of 'hound of Belenus', from *cú*, 'dog', a name borne by a first-century chieftain of South Britain who resisted the Roman invasion. An anglicised form is Cymbeline.

Curig (Welsh, male)
A Welsh saint, whose name is preserved in Capel Curig, Caernarvon, Llangurig, Montgomery, and other places.

Cuthbert *see* CATHBAD

Cymbeline *see* CUNOBELINUS

Cynan (Welsh, male) *Kee-nan*
The name of a thirteenth-century Welsh prince, Cynan ap Hywel.

Cynedda (Welsh, male) *Kee-netha*
A semi-legendary figure of the fifth century:
a king of the Britons of Strathclyde, who established their kingdom also in Gwynedd.

Cynddelw (Welsh, male) *Keen-dellow*
The name of a major twelfth-century poet.

Cynddylan (Welsh, male) *Keen-thilann*
A sixth-century prince of Powys.

Cynfab (Welsh, male) *Keen-fab*
'First son'.

Cynfael (Welsh, male) *Keen-file*
A warrior name, from *cyn*, 'chief'; *mael*, 'armour' or 'prince'.

Cynfrig (Welsh, male) *Keen-frec*
A river name, incorporating Welsh *cyn*,
'head', 'top'. Anglicised forms are Kendrick,
Kendrew.

Cynog (Welsh, male) *Kee-noc*
A sixth-century saint, whose name is preserved in numerous places including Llangynog and Ystradgynlais.

Cynon (Welsh, male)
Probably originally a river name, Afon Cynon, and incorporating Welsh *cynnig*, 'offer', suggesting a river that flowed by a chapel or place of offering (like the Scottish river Orrin) but could also derive from *cú*, 'hound', like many other names. Long in use as a personal name, and borne by many Old Welsh heroes.

D

Dafydd (Welsh, male) *Daf-ith*
The Welsh form of 'David'. Dafydd ap Gwilym
(fourteenth century) is one of Wales's greatest
poets. The one-time by-name for a Welshman,
'Taffy', comes from this name, because of its
frequency in earlier times. *See* DEWI, DEIAN, DAI.

Daibhidh (Scottish Gaelic, male)
A Gaelic form of David, and a name borne
by two Scottish kings.

Daimíne (Irish Gaelic, male) *Daa-win*
From *daimhín*, 'little fawn'. Anglicised as
Damien or Damian.

Dair (Scots, male)
This name may hark back to Gaelic *dar*, 'oak', or may simply be the latter part of ALASDAIR, originally an abbreviation, but turned into a separate name by the association with oak.

Dáire (Irish Gaelic, male) *Darr-ya*
'Fruitful', 'fertile'. A popular name in early Ireland. Dáire macFiachna was the owner of the famous Brown Bull of Cooley.

Dairean, Dáirine, Doiren, Doirend *see* DARINA

Dallas (Scottish Gaelic, male)
A location name and surname also found as a first name, from Gaelic *dail*, 'field', *eas*, 'falling stream'.

Daly (Irish, female)
This surname is also used as a first name; it derives from *dáil*, 'meeting', perhaps with the sense of 'counsellor'.

Damian, Damien *see* DAMÍNE

Dana (Irish Gaelic, female) *Daa-na*
This ancient name comes from a Celtic goddess, originally ANU or Ana, 'the abundant one'; the name later was modified to Danu, or Dana.

Danu *see* DANA

Dara (Irish Gaelic, female)
'Oak', from Gaelic *dar*, 'oak'. Another form of the same name is Deri. The oak was a venerated tree in Celtic lore, playing a part in the druidic cult.

Darby (Irish, male)
A shortened form of DIARMAID.

D'Arcy (Irish, female)
Properly a surname, of Norman-French origin, its use as a first name in Ireland may be influenced by its assimilation to Gaelic *dorcha*, 'dark'.

Darina (Irish, female)
A form of Gaelic *dáireann*, 'fruitful'. The Gaelic name is Dáirine, with alternative forms Daireann, Doirend, Doirenn. Darina Allen is one of Ireland's best-known cooks.

Darthula (English, female)
James Macpherson's adaptation of the name DEIRDRE in his Ossian poems.

David *see* DAFYDD, DAIBHIDH

Davidina *see* DAVINA

Davina (Scots, female)
A feminine form of David. But it could also be linked to *daimhin*, 'fawn'. Davidina is more unequivocal.

Dearbhail (Irish Gaelic, female) *Jerval*.
'Sincere'. The anglicised form is Dervla. Dervla Murphy is an intrepid and well-known travel writer.

Dearbhorgaill (Irish and Scottish Gaelic, female)
Jer-vor-gil
Perhaps stemming from the same root as
DEARBHAIL. Anglicised forms are Devorguilla,
Devorgilla. In Irish legend Devorguilla was
one of the many women to fall in love with
Cuchullain. Devorguilla Balliol, mother of
King John Balliol of Scotland, founded Balliol
College, Oxford, and Sweetheart Abbey in
Dumfries-shire.

Deasúin *see* DESMOND

Declan (Irish Gaelic, male)
The name of an early Celtic missionary who
preceded St Patrick to Ireland; perhaps stemming from Gaelic *deagh*, 'good'. The Gaelic
form is Deaglán.

Dechtire (Irish Gaelic, female) *Dec-tira*
Possibly stemming from Gaelic *deich*, 'ten'.
Dechtire, daughter of the druid Cathbad, was
the mother of CUCHULLAIN. Alternative forms

are Deichtine, Deicteir and the anglicised
Dectora.

Dee (Gaelic, Welsh, female)
This is a river name in Ireland, Wales, England
and Scotland, and as it derives from a root word
dia, 'goddess', is quite apt as a girl's name.

Dedwydd (Welsh, male) *Ded-with*
'Blessed one'.

Deian, Dai (Welsh, male)
Diminutive forms of DAFYDD.

Deiniol (Welsh, male)
Saint Deiniol is the founder of abbeys at Bangor, Caernarfon, and Bangor-on-Dee.

Deirdre (Irish Gaelic, female) *Deer-dra*
The source of the name is uncertain, but despite its legendary linking with 'sorrows', it
is unlikely to be anything to do with grief. It
may simply mean 'girl' or 'daughter'. The

name of the tragic heroine of a great poem from the *Ulster Cycle*, it is widely used in Ireland and Scotland.

Delwyn (Welsh, male)
'Pretty boy', from *del*, 'pretty'.

Delyth (Welsh, female) *Del-ith*
'Pretty girl', from *del*, 'pretty'.

Demelza (Cornish, female)
A Cornish placename, popularised as a first name by the heroine of Winston Graham's *Poldark* novels.

Dennis *see* DENZIL, DION

Denzil (Cornish, male)
A form of the Greek name Dionysius, whose anglicised form is Dennis.

Deórsa (Scottish Gaelic, male)
A Gaelic form of George. *See also* SEÓRAS.

Derfel (Welsh, male)
A saint's name, preserved at Llandderfel, Merioneth. The name also refers to a prophetic character portrayed in John Cowper Powys's novel *Owen Glendower*.

Deri (Welsh, male)
'Oak-like', from *derw*, 'oak tree'.

Dermot, Derry *see* DIARMAID

Derryth (Welsh, female)
A feminine form of DERI.

Desmond (Irish Gaelic, male)
From Gaelic *deas*, 'south', *Mumu*, 'Munster'. A territorial name associated especially with the Fitzgerald family. The modern Gaelic form is Deasúin.

Deva (Latin, female)
The Latinised form of the river name Dee, found in England, Ireland, Wales and Scotland.

Devorgilla, Devorguilla *See* DEARBHORGAILL

Dewi (Welsh, male)
A form of David. Dewi Sant, or St David, patron saint of Wales, died 588.

Diarmaid (Irish and Scottish Gaelic, male) *Der-mit*
'He who reverences God', from Gaelic *dia*, 'God'. The name of many heroes of legend, especially Diarmait úa Duibne, the hero of *The Pursuit of Diarmaid and Gráinne*. The last pagan high king of Ireland was said to be Diarmait macCearbhal (died *c.* 568). Alternative forms are Diarmuid, Diarmid, and the anglicised Dermot. A pet form is Derry.

Diarmait, Diarmit, Diarmuid *see* DIARMAID

Dilic (Cornish, female) *Dee-lik*
Perhaps an early saint's name.

Dilys (Welsh, female)
'Sincere'.

Dion (Welsh, male) *Dee-on*
A Welsh form of Dennis, which comes from Greek Dionysius.

Dod (Scots, male)
A pet form of George. Other pet forms are Dodie, Doddy.

Dogmael (Welsh, male) *Dog-mile*
St Dogmael is a Welsh saint, contemporary with St David.

Doirend *See* DARINA

Dolina (Scots, female) *Dol-eena*
A feminine form of Donald, common in Gaelic-speaking areas in the nineteenth and early twentieth centuries, and still in use. *See also* DONALDA.

Dolores *see* BRÓNAGH

Domhnall, Donal *see* DONALD

Donald (Scottish and Irish Gaelic, male)
The Gaelic form is Domhnall, from a Celtic root dubno or dumno, 'great ruler'. Nowadays mostly associated with Scotland, and once the most popular boys' name in the Highlands and Islands, but it was also a frequently used name in old Ireland and still used there in the form Donal. Pet forms include Don, Donnie.

Donaldina *see* DONALDA

Donalda (Scots, female)
A feminine form of Donald, usually given to the daughter of a man named Donald. Other feminine forms are Donaldina, Donella, DOLINA.

Donella *see* DONALDA

Donn (Irish and Scottish Gaelic)
'Brown', is the most common meaning attributed to this name, though Old Gaelic *donn* had a number of meanings including 'lord'.

Donnchadh *See* DUNCAN

Dorcas (English)
Not a Celtic name, but can be used as an anglicised form of Gaelic *dorchas*, 'dark'.

Dougal (Scottish Gaelic, male) *Doo-gal*
'Dark stranger', from Gaelic *dubh*, 'dark', and *gall*, 'stranger'. The Gaels differentiated between the Norwegians, 'fair strangers', and the Danes, 'dark strangers'. This name may have been given to a child with one Norse parent. It is often wrongly assumed to be cognate with Douglas, and the pet forms Doug, Dougie are the same in both. Alternative forms are Dugald, Dougall.

Dougald, Dougall *see* DOUGAL

Douglas (Scottish Gaelic, Manx, male) *Dugg-las*
'Dark water'. This was originally a location name from a place in the Scottish Borders, and the surname was adopted by twelfth-century

Flemish immigrants. The name achieved great fame with Sir James Douglas, comrade-in-arms of king Robert I. Pet forms are Doug, Dougie.

Douglasina (Scots, female)
A feminine form of Douglas.

Drostán (Irish Gaelic, male)
A follower of St Columba and founder of the monastery of Deer in Aberdeenshire.

Drudwen (Welsh, female)
'Precious'.

Drust (Pictish, male)
Name of several Pictish kings, including the eighth-century Drust, son of Talorcan. Alternative forms are Drustan, Drostan, perhaps commemorated in the hill Trostan in County Antrim.

Drustan (Brythonic, male)
This name is sometimes taken as an older version of TRYSTAN.

Dubh (Irish and Scottish Gaelic, female) *Doov*
'Dark one', from Gaelic *dubh*, 'black'.

Dubthach (Irish and Scottish Gaelic, male/female) *Doo-tach*
From Gaelic *dubh*, 'black'. Source of the Irish surname O'Duffy.

Duff (Scots, male)
Stemming from Gaelic *dubh*, 'dark', this is an ancient surname sometimes used as a first name.

Duncan (Scots, male)
'Brown warrior', from Gaelic *donn*, 'brown', and *cath*, 'warrior'. The Gaelic form is Donnchadh and in this form was popular in Gaelic Ireland as well as in Scotland. The first king of all Scotland was Duncan (*c.* 1001–1040). Duncan Bán MacIntyre was a famous Scottish Gaelic poet. Pet forms are Dunc, Dunkie.

Dungal (Scottish Gaelic, male) *Dunn-gal*, or *Dowall*
'Brown stranger', from Gaelic *donn*, 'brown', and *gall*, 'stranger'. Anglicised as Dowal, it is the source of the Galloway surname MacDowall.

Dyfri (Welsh, male) *Dee-fri*
The name of an early Welsh saint.

Dylan (Welsh, male)
'Son of the waves'. In the *Mabinogion* poems, the name of a son of Arianrod. Appropriately, it was borne by the poet Dylan Thomas (1914–1953).

Dymphna (Irish Gaelic, female)
This was the name of a seventh-century Irish saint. It may stem from Gaelic *dán*, 'poetry'.

E

Eachann (Scottish Gaelic, male) *Yach-ann.*
The Gaelic form of the name Hector. It is a
translation rather than a sound adaptation.
The derivation of Greek Hector is 'horse lord',
and this name stems from Gaelic each, 'horse'.

Eachna (Irish Gaelic, female) *Yach-na*
Probably a feminine form of Eachann. An alternative form is Echna.

Eadain *see* Etaín

Ealasaid (Scottish Gaelic) *Yalla-suth*
Gaelic form of Elizabeth.

Ealga (Irish Gaelic, female) *Yal-ga*
'Noble, brave'.

Eamair, Eamhair *see* EMER

Eamonn, Eamon (Irish Gaelic) *Ay-mon*
The Gaelic form of Edmund. Eamonn an Chnuic, 'of the hill', was a famous outlaw of the seventeenth century in County Tipperary. Eamon de Valera (1882–1975) was the first President of the Irish Republic.

Eanraig (Scottish Gaelic)
The Gaelic form of Henry.

Eavan (Irish Gaelic, female) *Ay-van*
A form of Gaelic AOIBHINN, 'radiant'.

Eber (Irish and Scottish Gaelic, male)
This was the name of the supposed founder of the Scots, great grandson of Scota, a daughter of the Pharaoh Nectanebo. Its etymology is uncertain. Another, later, Eber was a son of Míl Espáine (*see* MILES).

Edna *see* EITHNA

Ednyfed (Welsh, male) *Ed-niffith*
Ednyfed was a thirteenth-century king of Gwynnedd, but referred to in Thomas Love Peacock's poem 'The War Song of Dinas Vawr' as 'Ednyfed, king of Dyfed'.

Edain *see* ETAIN

Edna *see* EITHNA

Eevin *see* AÍBELL

Efa (Welsh, female)
The Welsh form of Eve.

Egan *see* AODHAGÁN

Eibhlinn (Irish and Scottish Gaelic, female) *Aivlinn*
The Gaelic Eibhlinn is related to *aoibhlinn*, 'radiance' and is the source of this name. In the course of time it has sometimes been taken as related to other names, including Eve and

103

Aveline. Its most common anglicised version is Eileen.

Eigra (Welsh, female) *Eye-gra*
'Fair maid'. Eigr was the reputed name of King ARTHUR's mother, found in Sir Thomas Malory's Arthurian tales as Igraine.

Eilidh (Irish and Scottish Gaelic) *Ay-lee*
Gaelic form of Helen. The name is originally Greek and means 'bright one'. A pet form is Ellie.

Eilis (Irish Gaelic, female)
Probably a Gaelicised form of Alice.

Eiluned *See* LUNED

Eilwen (Welsh, female) *Isle-wen*
'White-browed'.

Eimear, Eimer *see* EMER

Einion (Welsh, male) *Ine-yon*
'Anvil'. An often-found name in Welsh legend, anglicised into Eynon. *See* BEYNON.

Eira (Welsh, female) *Eye-ra*
'Snow'. Another form is Eirwen, equivalent to 'Snow-white'.

Eire (Irish Gaelic, female) *Ay-ra*
The name of an old Irish goddess which had become synonymous with the country of Ireland.

Eirian (Welsh, male/female) *Eye-reean*
'Fair, shining'. A girl-only form is Eirianwen.

Eirianwen *see* EIRIAN

Eiriol (Welsh, female) *Eye-reeol*
'Beseeching'.

Eirlys (Welsh, female) *Ire-lis*
'Snowdrop'.

Eirwen *see* Eira

Eirys (Welsh, female) *Iris*
Welsh form of 'Iris'.

Eithna (Irish Gaelic, female) *Eth-na*
Eithne was a goddess name which was also
held by some early Irish saints; it stems from
Gaelic eithne, 'kernel', implying both fertil-
ity and the heart of things. Other forms are
Eithne, Eithlenn, Enya, there is a Welsh form,
Ethni, and it is anglicised into Edna.

Elaine *See* Elen

Elan (Welsh, female)
A river name.

Elen (Welsh, female)
Welsh form of Helen. Elen was the virgin
princess in the *Dream of Macsen Wledig*; a tale
of the Roman governor Magnus Maximus
who tried to make himself Emperor of Rome.

An anglicised form is Elaine, name of 'the lily maid of Astolat' who fell in love with Sir Lancelot in the English Arthurian legend related by Sir Thomas Malory.

Eleri (Welsh, female)
Eleri was a daughter of the fifth-century chieftain BRYCHAN. It is also a river name from Ceredigion.

Elffin *see* ELPHIN

Elidir (Welsh, male)
The name of a legendary handsome boy, loved by the gods. Elidir was the father of Llywarch Hen (sixth century). An alternative form is Elidor.

Elinor (Welsh, female)
The Welsh form of Eleanor.

Elphin (Welsh, male)
This name may be from the same root as

Latin albus, 'white'. The name of a prover-
bially unlucky lad whose fortune changes
when he rescues and becomes foster father
to the baby Taliesin. An alternative form is
Elffin.

Elspeth (Scots, female)
A Scots form of Elizabeth. It is sometimes
shortened to the pet name Eppie.

Elwyn (Welsh, male)
Kind, fair, from *elus*, 'kind', and *gwyn*, 'fair'.

Elystan (Welsh, male)
Welsh form of Old English Athelstan.

Emer (Irish Gaelic, female) *Ay-mer*
The name of the wife of the great legendary
hero CUCHULLAIN. Other forms are Eamair,
Eimear, Eimer, and, in Scotland, Eamhair.
Emer was said to possess all six gifts of wom-
anhood: beauty, chastity, soft voice, clear
speech, skill with the needle, and wisdom.

Emergaid (Manx, female) *Aymer-gatt*
The name of a legendary princess of Man.

Emlyn (Welsh, male)
A Welsh form of the Latin name Aemilius.

Emrys (Welsh, male) *Em-riss*
The Welsh form of Ambrose, Latin Ambrosius, who as one of the Fathers of the Church was widely venerated beyond his territory of Lombardy. Emrys Wledig, 'prince', was the Welsh name of Ambrosius Aurelianus, leader of the Britons against the invading Saxons in the fifth century AD. Emrys Hughes was a fiery twentieth-century Labour MP.

Emyr (Welsh, male)
Emyr Llydaw was a sixth-century saint. Emyr Humphreys was a well-known twentieth-century writer.

Ena (Irish, Scots, female)
So many girl names end in -ina or -ena that

this suffix may have taken on a life of its own as a girl's name. It may also be a form of Gaelic Eithne, 'kernel'.

Enda (Irish Gaelic, male)
It is not uncommon for boys' names in Gaelic to end in -a, and St Enda or Enna, was a sixth-century holy man, founder of a monastery on the Aran Islands, his name derived perhaps from Gaelic *éan*, 'bird'.

Endellion (Cornish, female)
The original form of the name was Endelient, preserved in St Endellion, a legendary saint of the fifth century who eschewed all food and lived on milk and water.

Enid (Welsh, female)
Enid is a name from the Arthurian legends, derived from Welsh *enaid*, 'soul'.

Enya *see* Eithna

Eocha, Eochai, Eochaid, Eochy *see* Eochaidh

Eochaidh (Irish Gaelic, male) *Yoch-ee*
From Gaelic *each*, 'horse', probably inferring 'horse-master' (*see* EACHANN). A very frequent name in old Irish legends and histories. Eochaidh was the name of an ancient sun-god, said to be the possessor of a single red eye. Eochaidh Airem, 'ploughman', was a legendary high king, earthly lover of the beautiful ETAÍN. The name was also used by the Picts. Alternative forms are Eocha, Eochaid, Eochai, Eochy.

Eoganán (Irish and Scottish Gaelic, male) *Yo-hanann*
One of the seven sons of Oengus (*see* ANGUS), all of whom were holy men of the sixth century. But the name, stemming back to Celtic *eo*, 'yew', is suggestive of tree worship in an earlier period. Also found as Eogan, Eoghan. Anglicised forms are Eugene and Owen, both unconnected with the Celtic etymology of the name.

Eoghan *See* EOGANÁN, EWAN

Eoin (Irish Gaelic, male) *Yonn*
A Gaelic form of John. Eoin macSuibhne was
a chieftain of Ulster in the early fourteenth
century. *See also* IAIN, SEAN.

Eolas (Irish Gaelic, male/female) *Yo-las*.
'Knowledge', 'experience'.

Erc (Irish Gaelic, male)
From Old Gaelic *earc*, 'speckled'. Erc was the
father of Fergus, Angus and Loarn, first lords
of Gaelic Dalriada. Erc macTelt is recorded
as the ultimate ancestor of the Clan Cameron.

Ercol (Irish Gaelic, male)
Perhaps combining Gaelic *earc*, 'speckled',
and *col*, 'lord', though its resemblance to
Greek Hercules has also been noted. It was
the name of a Connacht warrior, humbled by
CUCHULAINN.

Erin (Irish Gaelic, female)
A form of Eire, also found as Eriu.

Ernan *See* IARNAN

Erne (Irish Gaelic, female) *Er-na*
Name of a legendary princess, preserved in
Lough Erne.

Ertha (Cornish, female)
The name of an early Celtic saint.

Essyllt *See* ISEULT

Etaín (Irish Gaelic, female) *Ithoyne*
A name from Old Irish mythology. Etaín was
the second wife of MIDIR, but was changed
into a fly, and swallowed by a woman who
then gave birth to a 'new' Etaín who married
King EOCHAIDH, but was eventually reclaimed
by Midir and brought back to the 'Land of
Many Colours'. Her name is synonymous
with feminine beauty. Alternative forms are
Etáin, Edaín, Eadain. The name is sometimes
anglicised to Aideen.

Ethna *see* EITHNA

Euan *see* E<small>WAN</small>

Eurfron (Welsh, female) *Ire-fronn*
'Golden-breasted'. From *aur*, 'gold'.

Eurig (Welsh, male) *Eye-ric*
'Golden'.

Euron (Welsh, female) *Eye-ronn*
'Golden one'. This was the name of the be-
loved of the bard Iolo Morgannwg.

Eurwen (Welsh, female)
'Fair, golden', from *aur*, 'gold', and *ven*,
'white'.

Eurwyn (Welsh, male) *Ire-win*
'Fair, golden;' masculine form of Eurwen.

Eva *see* A<small>OIFE</small>

Evan (Welsh, male)
A Welsh form of John.

Evelyn *see* AIBHLINN

Everett *see* AEBRIC

Evric *see* AEBRIC

Ewan (Scots, male) *Yoo-wan*
An anglicised form of Gaelic Eoghan. Other forms include Euan, Ewen, Evan.

Ewen *see* EWAN

Eynon *see* EINON

F

Fand (Irish Gaelic, female)
From Old Irish *fand*, 'tear'. A beautiful heroine of legend.

Faolán (Irish Gaelic, male)
'Wolf-like'. From *faolán*, 'wolf'. This was a term of praise rather than denigration. The name was borne by an Irish missionary to Scotland, and is preserved in the village name St Fillans.

Farquhar (Scots, male) *Farr-char*
Anglicised form of Gaelic Fearchar, from Old Gaelic *ver-car-os*, 'very dear one'.

Fay (Irish, Scots, female)
The source of this name is not clear; it has associations with English 'Faith', though there is also a Gaelic root *fei*, 'faith'. There is also a possible connection with French *fée*, witch or wise woman, *fay* in Norman French, and English 'fairy'. An alternative form is Faye.

Faye *see* FAY

Féchin (Irish Gaelic, male) *Fay-hin*
From Gaelic *fiach*, 'raven'. A name borne by numerous early saints. Alternative forms are Féchine, Féichin. *See also* FIACHRA.

Féchine *see* FÉCHIN

Fedelm *see* FIDELMA

Fedlimid (Irish Gaelic, male/female) *Fellimy*
Of unclear derivation, a name found often in ancient sources, occasionally as a female

118

name. Other forms include Fedelmid, Feidhlimidh, Feidhlim, and anglicised Felim or Felimy.

Fedelmid *see* FEDELIMID

Feichin *see* FÉCHIN

Feidhilim, Feidhlimidh, Felim, Felimy *see* FEDELIMID

Fenella *see* FIONNUALA

Fearchar *see* FARQUHAR

Ferdia, Ferdiad (Irish Gaelic, male)
The name has been derived from Gaelic *fear*, 'man', and *dia*, 'god', but if so it is a pre-Christian god; also from *diad*, 'smoke' Ferdia or Ferdiad was the brother-in-arms of CUCHULAINN, but whom Cuchulainn slew in single combat.

Fergal (Irish Gaelic, male)
Derived from *fearghal*, 'brave'.

Fergus (Irish Gaelic, male)
The name has been derived as 'best warrior', from Gaelic *fearr*, 'best', and *gas*, 'warrior', or 'only choice' from an older Celtic root, *ver gustu*; though another possibility is 'virile man'. Fergus was a legendary king of Ulster who was supplanted by CONCHOBHAR and so supported Queen Medb in her famous 'Cattle Raid', and the name was borne by many others including Fergus Mór macErc, founder of the kingdom of Dalriada in Scotland. Pet forms include Ferg, Fergie.

Ffion (Welsh, female)
A flower name, 'rose' or 'foxglove finger'.

Ffraid (Welsh, female) *Fryde*
Welsh form of Bride (*see* BRÍD), found in numerous placenames.

Fiachna (Irish Gaelic, male)
From *fiach*, 'raven'. This name and FIACHRA are often confused.

Fiachra (Irish Gaelic, male)
From *fiach*, 'raven'. St Fiachra was a seventh-century Celtic saint whose name is preserved in French in St Fiacre and the Fiacre or horse-drawn cab.

Fianaid (Irish Gaelic, female) *Fee-ana*
'Little deer'.

Fidelma (Irish Gaelic)
Fedelm was the prophetess who warned Queen Medb of the coming rout of her army in the Cattle Raid of Cooley. The name has also been borne by a number of Celtic saints and though its origin is obscure, clearly indicates a person of spiritual force.

Fillan *See* FAOLÁN

Finegin *see* FINGEIN

Finella *See* FIONNUALA

Finán (Scottish and Irish Gaelic, male) *Fin-ann*
The name of several early saints of the Celtic church.

Finbar *see* FINBARR

Finbarr (Irish Gaelic, male)
St Finbarr of Cork was widely venerated in the Celtic lands. The likely derivation of the name is *fionn*, 'white', and *barr*, 'head, crest': the fair-haired one. Alternative forms include Finnbarr, Findbarr, Finbar. *See* BARRFIND.

Findbarr *see* FINBARR

Fingal (Scottish Gaelic, male)
'Fair stranger', from *fionn*, 'white, fair', and *gall*, 'stranger'. A name given to Norsemen by the Celts. In Scotland however it is also a name

given to FIONN macCumhaill, at least since the fourteenth century, and perpetuated in 'Fingal's Cave' (although this name was not given to the 'cave of music' until the eighteenth century).

Fingein (Irish Gaelic, male)
'Wine birth'. A common name in old Irish sources. Variant forms include Finegin, Finghean, and anglicised Finnigan.

Finghean *see* FINGEIN

Fingon (Scottish Gaelic, male)
A form of Fingein.

Finn *See* FIONN

Finlay (Scots, male) *Finn-la*
From Gaelic *fionn*, 'fair', and laoch, 'hero', 'warrior'.

Finnabair (Irish Gaelic, female) *Finna-warr*
'Fair-browed'. The name of MEDB's daugh-

ter, lover of Fráech (*see* FRAOCH), who died with grief when he was killed by CUCHULAINN. The name is related to Welsh GWENHWYFAR.

Finnán (Irish and Scottish Gaelic, male)
'Little fair one', from *fionn*, 'fair', with the diminutive ending -an. *See also* FINNIAN.

Finnbar *see* FINBARR

Finnbheara (Irish Gaelic, male) *Finn-waira*
The name of a fairy king of Connaught.

Finnegas, Finegas (Irish Gaelic, male)
From *fionn*, 'fair', and *geas*, 'warrior', this was the name of the tutor of FIONN macCumhaill. Finnegas sought to catch the magic salmon of all knowledge, and did so, but his pupil touched the fish, sucked his finger, and acquired the knowledge.

Finnghuala *See* FIONNUALA

Finnian (Irish and Scottish Gaelic, male)
The derivation is the same as that of FINNÁN,
and the two names have often been confused.
St Finnian of Clonard (sixth century) is the
best-known bearer of the name.

Finnigan *see* FINGEIN

Fintan (Irish Gaelic, male)
One of the many names incorporating *fionn*,
'white, fair'; the other element has been construed both as 'ancient' and as 'fire'. There
were many St Fintans in the Celtic church,
but it goes back into ancient legend as the
name of the salmon of knowledge. In another
legend, Fintan macBochra was the only Irish-
man to survive Noah's flood.

Fiona (Scots, female)
Though Gaelic in appearance, this is a rela-
tively modern 'artificial' name, though very
popular. It recalls Gaelic *fionn*, 'white,' a con-
stituent of many names.

Fionn (Irish and Scottish Gaelic, male) *Fin*
'Fair, bright', meaning fair-haired. This was
the name of one of the greatest figures of
Celtic legend, the mighty warrior, wise man
and bard FIONN macCumhaill, the leader of
the Fianna. In Northern Scotland Finn is also
a Norse name, from a different root. *See also*
FINGAL.

Fionnuala (Irish Gaelic, female) *Finn-oola*
Fionnuala was one of the four children, and
only daughter of king Lír and his wife AOBH,
all of whom were transformed by enchant-
ment into swans. The name steams from
Gaelic *fionn*, 'white', and *ghuala*, 'shoulders'.
Alternate forms include Fionola, Finola, and
the anglicised Fenella. *See also* NUALA

Flann (Irish Gaelic, male/female)
'Red'. This ancient name became famous in
the later twentieth century as a pen-name
of Brian O'Nolan, who wrote as Flann
O'Brien.

Flora (Scots, female)
Though Latin in origin, meaning 'flower', this name has strong Celtic associations through Flora MacDonald (1722–1790), who aided Prince Charles Edward Stewart in his escape after the failure of the 1745–46 uprising and became a heroine among the Gaels and even among those who opposed the rising.

Florence (Irish, male)
The use of this name – usually a female one – for a boy seems to stem from an anglicisation of Fursa, which may have been supposed to be linked to Italian, Firenze. A pet form was Flurry. In Somerville and Ross's *Irish R.M.* stories, Flurry Knox was a 'gentleman among stable-boys and a stableboy among gentlemen'.

Floyd (English)
An anglicised version of Llwyd, or Lloyd. 'Pretty Boy Floyd' is a popular American folk song.

Flurry *see* FLORENCE

Fódla (Irish Gaelic, female) *Foh-la*
A land goddess name, synonymous with Ireland, like ERIN and BANBA. In one tradition these three were sisters.

Forbes (Scots, male)
Originally an Aberdeenshire surname, from Old Gaelic *forba*, 'field'.

Fráech *see* FRAOCH

Fraoch (Irish and Scottish Gaelic, male) *Fraach*
'Heath'. Although 'Heather' is today a girls' name, Fraoch was a male warrior. An alternative form is Fráech.

Fraser (Scots, male)
A surname often used as a first name. In Gaelic it is Friseil, derived perhaps from Old French *fraise*, 'strawberry', or from Frisian *frisel*, 'Frisian'.

Fursa (Irish Gaelic, male)
Of uncertain derivation, this name was borne
by a number of Celtic saints, most notably
Saint Fursa who had ecstatic and terrifying
visions, the account of which is said to have
inspired Dante to write his *Inferno*. The anglicised form is Fursey. *See* FLORENCE.

Fursey *see* FURSA

Fychan (Welsh, male) *Fee-han*
'Vaughan'.

G

Gabrán (Scottish Gaelic, male) *Gaw-ran*
Name of a Dalriadic king, perhaps linked
with Gaelic *gabhar*, 'goat'. The name is preserved in the Gowrie district of Angus.

Gaenor (Welsh, female)
Abbreviated form of GWENHWYFAR. Also found
in anglicised form as Gaynor.

Gael (Irish and Scottish Gaelic, female)
A Gael, Gaelic Gaidheal, is a Gaelic speaker;
this modern name is also seen in the forms
Gail, Gayle. Kylie is also a possible version.

Galvin (Irish Gaelic, female/male)
The source of this name has been traced to
Gaelic *geal*, 'white', and *fionn*, 'bright'; also
to *gealbhan*, 'sparrow'. It may equally well be
a form of GAWAIN.

Garaidh *see* GARETH

Gareth (Welsh, male)
A form of GERAINT. In the Arthurian legend
of the Round Table, Sir Gareth is the younger
brother of Sir Gawaine and Sir Gaheris. His
nickname in the English versions was
'Beaumains' or 'fine hands', and the name
was once taken to stem from Welsh *gwared*,
'mild, gentle', but this is now not accepted.
An Irish form of it is Garaidh.

Garret *See* GEARÓID

Garry (Scots, male)
A river name that is sometimes used as a first
name.

Gartnait (Pictish, male)
Of uncertain derivation, this was a common name in the Pictish kingdom and was preserved in the familty of the earls of Huntly. Another form is Garnaid, and though it could be anglicised as Garnet, there is no etymological connection.

Gavin *See* Gawain

Gawain (Welsh, male)
'White hawk', from *gwalch*, 'falcon', *gwyn*, 'white'. The Welsh form is Gwalchgwyn, and is taken to be the same name as Gwalchmai. Sir Gawain of Malory's Arthurian romance is known in Welsh as Gwalchmai fab Gwyar. As the principal knight of King Arthur he had great prestige and the name was adopted in Ireland and Scotland as Gavan, Gavin. His parents Lot and Morgause were said to be from Lothian and Orkney (the latter being part of the Pictish kingdom until the ninth-century Viking conquest).

Gay (Irish Gaelic, male)
'Spear', from Gaelic *gáe*, 'spear'. Spears were highly significant weapons to the Celts. This name can also be a shortened form of Gabriel, a non-Celtic name.

Gaynor *See* GWENHWYFAR

Gearóid (Irish Gaelic, male) *Garr-rode*
The Gaelic form of Gerald. The anglicised form is Garret. The name is closely linked to the Fitzgerald family, notably in the person of the fourteenth century third earl of Desmond, the magic-working Gearóid Iarla, 'Earl Gerald', and in the twentieth century by the Irish statesman Garret Fitzgerald.

Gearóidin (Irish Gaelic, female) *Garr-roh-din*
The Gaelic form of Geraldine, a Norman surname familiar in Ireland.

Geordie (Scots, male)
A pet form of George.

George *see* GEORDIE, DOD

Geraint (Welsh, male)
A Welsh form of the Latin name Gerontius.
The name of the warlike hero of the Welsh
Arthurian tale *Geraint and* ENID.

Gerald *see* GEARÓID, GERALT

Geraldine *see* GEARÓDIN

Geralt (Welsh, male)
The Welsh form of 'Gerald'. The ecclesiastic
Giraldus Cambrensis (Gerald the Welshman)
wrote extensively about life in the Celtic
world in his own era (thirteenth century) and
its earlier history.

Gethin (Welsh, male)
'Dark', from *cethin*, 'dusky, dark'.

Gilchrist (Scottish Gaelic, male)
'Servant or follower of Christ', from *gille*, 'follower'.

135

Gildas (Welsh, male)

Name of an ecclesiastic and historian, a contemporary of St David, said to have been born in the kingdom of Strathclyde, and author of *De Excidio Britanniae*, a description of the Saxon conquest of Britain. The name is found in Brittany as Gueltaz.

Giles (English, male)

Not of Celtic origin, the name comes from Greek *aigidion*, 'young goat', referring to the goatskin mantle of the saint. As the name of the patron of Edinburgh's high kirk, the name has some following in Scotland, where it also gains a Gaelic resonance from its resemblance to Gaelic *gille*, 'boy'.

Gilleasbuig (Scottish Gaelic, male) *Gheel-espic*

'Servant of the bishop', from Gaelic *gille*, 'servant'. In the past it was assumed to be a Gaelic version of Archibald ('bald' implying a clerical tonsure), resulting in numerous

Gilleasbuigs anglicising their names to this, instead of the more usual Gillespie.

Gillespie *See* Gilleasbuig

Gilmour (Scottish Gaelic, male)
'Follower of Mary', from *gille*, 'follower', *Mhuire*, 'of Mary'. The name of a priest originally.

Giorsail (Scottish Gaelic, female) *Ghee-orrsal* 'Grace'.

Gladys *See* Gwladys

Glanmor (Welsh, male)
'Clean or bright', and 'great'.

Glen (Scottish Gaelic, male)
From *gleann*, 'mountain valley'. Also found as Glenn.

Glenda (Welsh, female)
'Good, holy'.

Glenys (Welsh, female)
'Holy, fair one'. From the Welsh, *glân*, meaning 'pure, holy and fair'.

Glyn (Welsh, male)
Glyn is Welsh for 'valley', and originally indicated 'man of the valley'.

Glynis (Welsh, female)
The stem of this may be *glân*, as in Glenys; or it may be *glyn*, 'valley', indicating 'girl of the valley'.

Gofannon (Welsh, male)
'Smith', from *gofan*, 'smith'. The name of a legendary blacksmith.

Goll (Irish Gaelic, male)
'One-eyed'. The best known bearer of this name is Goll macMorna, opponent of Fionn macCumhaill in his bid to lead the Fianna.

Gomer (Welsh, male)
In Welsh legend, Gomer is the grandson of
Noah and progenitor of the Welsh people.

Gordon (Scots, male)
Originally a location name, Old Gaelic *gor
dun*, 'hill fort', from the Scottish Borders, it
became a family name and transferred with
the family to Strathbogie in North-east Scotland. Pet forms are Gord, Gordie.

Gormflath (Irish Gaelic, female) *Gorrum-la*
'Illustrious ruler', from Gaelic *gorm*, 'illustrious' (and also 'blue') and *flaith*, 'sovereignty'.
The name of numerous princesses and holy
women; the best known is the wife of Brian
Ború, a powerful dynastic figure in her own
right.

Goronwy (Welsh, male)
This name was popularised by Goronwy
Owen, the Anglesey bard (1723–1769).

Graeme (Scots, male) *Graym*
Originally a location name, either from Grantham in England or from Scots *gray hame*, 'grey house', this became a surname and then also a first name. Other forms are Graham, Grahame.

Graham, Grahame *see* GRAEME

Gráinne (Irish Gaelic, female) *Grawn-ya*
The name may come from *grán*, 'grain', suggesting an ancient fertility goddess; it has also been construed as 'she who terrifies'. A name from Irish legend; its most famous bearer was the Gráinne who was intended for marriage to the elderly FIONN macCumhaill but rebelled and eloped with Diarmaid his nephew, as told in *The Pursuit of Diairmaid and Gráinne*.

Grant (Scots, male)
From Old French *grand*, 'tall', this surname of twelfth-century Norman-French immigrants to the Badenoch district is now often used as a first name.

Granuaile (Irish Gaelic, female) *Grawn-walya*
Granuaile Mhaol, 'of the cropped hair'. Name
of the sixteenth-century 'pirate queen' of Connaught, also known as GRÁINNE, or in English form Grace O' Malley.

Greer (Scots, female)
A shortened form of Gregor (*see* GRIGOR).

Greg, Gregor, Gregory *see* GRIGOR

Griffith *see* GRUFFYDD

Grigor[1] (Pictish, Scottish Gaelic, male)
Girig was the name of more than one Pictish
king; the name stems from Old Gaelic *giric*,
'king's crest'. It has also picked up associations with Gregory, from Latin *gregorius*,
'watchman', a name given prestige by its links
with saints and popes. An alternative form is
Gregor; the pet version is Greg.

Grigor[2] (Welsh, male)
A form of Gregory.

Gruffudd *see* G<small>RUFFYDD</small>

Gruffydd (Welsh, male) *Griffith*
Anglicised as Griffith, this is a great name from Welsh history. Gruffydd ap Llewellyn was an eleventh-century ruler of Wales. Also spelt Gruffudd.

Gruoch (Pictish, female)
This was the name of Macbeth's queen, herself a woman of royal descent. The derivation is uncertain.

Gueltaz *see* G<small>ILDAS</small>

Guaire (Irish Gaelic, male) *Gwarr-ya*
From Gaelic *guaire*, 'noble', 'proud'. Guaire Aidne was a seventh-century king of Connacht.

Guinevere *see* G<small>WENHWYFAR</small>

Gwalchgwyn *see* G<small>AWAIN</small>

Gwalchmai (Welsh, male)
'Falcon of May', from *gwalch*, 'falcon', *mai*, 'May'. The latter part may alternatively mean 'of the plain', from Gaelic *maigh*. Gwalchmai fab Meilir was a poet of the twelfth century. *See* GAWAIN.

Gwatcyn (Welsh, male)
A Welsh form of Watkin, 'Little Walter'.

Gwaun (Welsh, male)
'Heath'.

Gwen (Welsh, female)
Abbreviated form of either GWENHWYFAR or of other names beginning in Gwen-, but also found on its own. From *wen*, 'white, fair'.

Gwenda (Welsh, female)
'Fair, good'.

Gwenhwyfar (Welsh, female) *Gwen iff-ar*
The name of Arthur's queen and found in

many legends. It stems from *gwyn*, 'white', and *hwyfar*, 'smooth'. Its earliest anglicised form was Guinevere, but it is much more frequently found as Jennifer. Other forms include Gaynor and the abbreviated Gwen.

Gwendolen (Welsh, female)
'Blessed, fair'. Often anglicised as Gwendoline.

Gwenonwyn (Welsh, female)
'Lily of the valley'.

Gwenydd (Welsh, female) *Gwen-ith.*
'Morning Star'.

Gwenfron (Welsh, female)
'Fair-breasted'.

Gwenllian (Welsh, female) *Gwen-hleean.*
'Fair, flaxen-haired'.

Gwennan (Welsh, female)
'Fair, blessed'.

Gwili (Welsh, male)
River name from Carmarthen, but perhaps also seen as a shortened form of GWILYM.

Gwilym (Welsh, male)
Welsh form of William.

Gwion (Welsh, male)
The boyhood name of TALIESIN the minstrel; also subject of the poem 'Gwion Bach'.

Gwladys, Gwladus (Welsh, female) *Glad-iss*
'Ruler'. Gwladus Ddu was the daughter of Llywelyn the Great. The anglicised form is Gladys.

Gwydion (Welsh, male)
The name of a powerful sorcerer, from the *Mabinogion* cycle of legends.

Gwylan (Welsh, female)
'Seagull'.

Gwyn (Welsh, male)
'White, blessed'. Gwyn ap Nudd was a legendary Welsh god, king of the 'Otherworld', Annwn.

Gwyneth (Welsh, female)
From the name of the old province and modern county of Gwynedd.

Gwynfor (Welsh, male)
'Bright lord'. From *gwyn*, 'white', and *ior*, 'lord'. Gwynfor Evans was for many years leader of Plaid Cymru, the Welsh National Party.

H

Hafwen (Welsh, female)
'Bright summer', from *haf*, 'summer', and
wen, 'fair'.

Hamish (Scots, male)
An anglicised version of Gaelic Seumas,
James, in its vocative form, A Seamuis.

Harvey (Breton, male)
Of Breton origin, and perhaps meaning 'bat-
tle-worthy'. The French form is Hervé.

Hazel (English, female)
Not a Celtic name (from Old English *haesel*),
but the hazel tree is important in Celtic lore

and tradition. Its twigs are used as divining rods and it was considered a fairy tree in Ireland and Wales.

Heilyn (Welsh, male) *Hye-lin*
'Cup-bearer'.

Heather (English, female)
First used as a girl's name in the nineteenth century, at a time when plant and flower names were very much in vogue.

Hergest (Welsh, male)
From the Radnor placename. *The Red Book of Hergest* is an early (sixth century) source of Welsh verse.

Hugh (English, male)
Not a Celtic name, though popular in the Celtic countries both in this and in Celtic forms. Often taken as an anglicised form of AED. *See also* HUW, UISDEAN.

Hughina (Scots, female)
A typically Highland girl's name, for a daughter of HUGH.

Huw (Welsh, male) *Hyoo*
Welsh form of HUGH.

Hywel (Welsh, male) *How-el*
'Outstanding, eminent'. Hywel Dda, 'the good', was a tenth-century Welsh king, famous for setting up a system of laws.

I

Iago (Welsh, male)
Welsh form of James, from Latin Jacobus.

Iain (Scots Gaelic, male) *Ee-yann*
The Scottish Gaelic form of John. The anglicised version Ian is also very popular.

Ianto (Welsh, male)
A pet form of IFAN.

Iarlaith (Irish Gaelic, male) *Yarr-la*
From *iarl*, 'knight'. The name of a fifth-century Irish saint. The anglicised form is Jarlath.

Iarnan (Irish and Scottish Gaelic) *Yarr-nan*
'Iron man', from Gaelic *iarann*, 'iron', indicating strength and fixity of purpose. St Iarnan was an uncle of St Columba. His name is preserved in Killearnan, on the Black Isle in Scotland.

Ida *see* IDE

Ide (Irish Gaelic, female) *Ee-ja*
Old Irish *íde*, 'thirst', means in this case thirst for virtue and knowledge, and was the name of St Ide. It is anglicised to Ida, though in this form it can also derive from other sources including Greek.

Idris (Welsh, male)
Idris Gawr was a legendary figure from around the seventh century, who has given his name to Cader Idris (Idris's Fort), a mountain in Merioneth.

Idwal (Welsh, male)
'Lord of the ramparts'. From *iud*, 'lord'.

Iestyn (Welsh, male)
A Welsh form of Justin.

Ieuan (Welsh, male)
A Welsh form of John.

Ifan (Welsh, male) *Ee-fan*
A Welsh form of John.

Ifor (Welsh, male)
A Welsh form of Ivor.

Igraine (Cornish, female)
This was the name of the mother of King ARTHUR. Wife of Gorlois, duke of Cornwall, she conceived Arthur by UTHER Pendragon, whom she married after Gorlois's death in battle. Variants are Igerna, Ygraine, Yguerne. *See* EIGRA.

Illtyd (Welsh, male) *Ll-tood*
From *iud*, 'lord', probably meaning 'lord of all' (*see* DONALD). A Welsh saint of the fifth

century, whose name is preserved in Llantwit Major, in Glamorgan.

Imogen (English, female) *Immo-genn*
This name, from Shakespeare's play *Cymbeline* is altered from Innogen, which probably has the same source as Gaelic *nighean*, 'daughter, girl'.

Indulf (Pictish, male)
The name of more than one Pictish king.

Ineda (Cornish, female) *Inn-ida*
The name of a Celtic saint, possibly confused with St Enda. The derivation seems to be the same as that of Enda.

Innes (Scottish Gaelic, male)
A surname occasionally used as a first name. It means 'island or meadow-dweller', from Gaelic *inis*, 'island, water-meadow'.

Innogen *see* IMOGEN

Ioan (Welsh, male)
One of the Welsh forms of John.

Iolo (Welsh, male)
An abbreviation of Iorwerth. Iolo Goch, the bard, was an associate of Owain Glyndwr; another bard, Iolo Morgannwg (1747–1826) created the *Gorsedd of Bards*.

Iona (Scots, female)
The name of the holy island is a popular one for girls. It is actually a medieval mis-reading of the original name, Ioua, perhaps meaning 'island of yews'.

Iorweth (Welsh, male)
'Worthy lord'. An alternative, usually found as a surname, is Yorath.

Iseabeal (Irish Gaelic, female) *Eesh-aval*
Gaelic form of Isabel, itself a Spanish form of Elizabeth.

Ishbel (Scots, female)
A form of Isabel, based on the Gaelic pronunciation. *See* ISEABEAL.

Iseult (Cornish/Welsh, female)
'Fair to look on'. There are two famous Iseults in the Arthurian legends, Iseult of Ireland, the true lover of TRISTAN, and Iseult 'of the White Hands' of Brittany, who deceives him into thinking she is the other. Alternative forms are Isolde, Isoult, Yseult, Essyllt.

Isla (Scots, female) *Eye-la*
A river name from Perthshire, in use as a first name since the nineteenth century.

Islay (Scots, male) *Eye-la*
The name of an island of the Inner Hebrides; as a personal name it is almost exclusively associated with Clan Campbell.

Isolde *see* ISEULT

Ivàr (Scots, male)
From an Old Norse personal name, Ivar, adopted into Gaelic as Iomhar. An alternative form is Ivor.

Ivor *see* IVAR, IFOR

J

James (Scots, male)
Though not Celtic in its origin (from Latin Jacobus), it has strong Scottish associations, with six Scottish kings bearing the name. The pet forms Jaikie, JAMIE and Jimmy are distinctively Scots.

Jamesina (Scots, female)
Another example of the once-common practice of tacking -ina on to a father's name.

Jamie (Scots, male/female)
This pet form of James has taken off as a name in its own right, and is often given to girls, as with the American actress Jamie Lee Curtis.

Jarlath *see* IARLAITH

Jean (Scots, female)
A feminine form of John, from Old French, Jehane. This was once one of the most frequent girls' names in Scotland. Robert Burns wrote many love poems to his wife Jean Armour. The pet form is Jeannie.

Jenkin *See* SIENCYN

Jennifer (Cornish, female)
Cornish form of GWENHWYFAR.

Jock (Scots, male)
A pet form of John. When John was the most popular boys' name, Jock became synonymous with 'Scotsman'. It has a pet form of its own, Jocky.

John *see* EVAN, IAIN, IEUAN, IFAN, IOAN, JOCK, SEAN, SIENCYN, SION, YANN

K

Kady (Irish Gaelic, female)
Perhaps influenced by Katie, but the name
could stem from Gaelic *céadach*, 'first'.

Karadoc (Breton, male)
A Breton form of CARADOG.

Karel (Breton, female)
A form of Carol, feminine form of Charles,
from Old German *carl*, 'man'.

Karen *see* CAIRENN

Kathleen *See* CAITLÍN

Kay (English, male/female)
The foster-brother and seneschal of King ARTHUR in the English Arthurian legends. *See* CEI. As a girls' name, Kay is a shortened form of Catherine or Katherine.

Kaylin *see* CAOILFHINN

Keelan, Keelin *see* CÁELFIND

Keera *see* CIARA

Keeva *see* KEVA

Keir (Scots, male)
From Gaelic *ciar*, 'dark'. Another form is Kerr. See also CIARÁN, KIERAN

Keira *see* CIARA

Keith (Scottish Gaelic, male) *Keeth*
Probably from Old Gaelic *coit*, 'wood', though it has also been associated with Cait, one of the seven sons of CRUITHNE, father of the Picts.

Kelly (Irish Gaelic, male/female)
The source of the name is *cill*, 'church', and it
indicated a special supporter of the church.
See also CEALLACH.

Kelvin (Scots, male)
From the Glasgow river, whose name stems
from Gaelic *caol*, 'narrow', and *abhainn*,
'stream'.

Kendrew, Kendrick *see* CYNFRIG

Kennedy (Scots-Irish, male)
Originally a nickname, from Gaelic *ceann*,
'head', *eidhigh*, 'ugly'; this name is associated
with South-west Scotland and Ireland.

Kenneth (Scots, male)
'Handsome'. From Gaelic *coinneach*, 'hand-
some'. As the name of a saint and of the first
king of the united Picts and Scots, Kenneth
MacAlpin, it had great prestige. Pet forms are
Ken, Kenny.

Kentigern (Brythonic, male)
Probably meaning 'of royal descent', from Welsh *teyrn*, 'king', this was the name of the Celtic missionary who became Glasgow's patron saint. *See also* MUNGO.

Kerr *see* KEIR, CIARAN

Kerry (Irish Gaelic, female/male)
Name of the Irish county, probably stemming from Gaelic *ciar*, 'dark', suggesting 'land of the dark (haired) people'. Now widely used without any direct connection to the area.

Keva (Irish, female)
An anglicised form of Gaelic Caoimhe, an old name indicating 'beauty', 'grace'. Keeva is an alternative form.

Keverne (Cornish, male)
Anglicised version of a Cornish form of KEVIN.

Kevin (Irish, male)
From Gaelic *caomhin*, 'born handsome', and

made popular by the story of Saint Kevin of Glendalough (died around AD 620), celebrated for his chastity and devotion. This name spread from Ireland in the twentieth century to be a popular one throughout the English-speaking world.

Kiera (Irish, female) *Kee-ra*
A feminine version of KIERAN.

Kieran (Irish Gaelic, male)
An anglicised form of CIARÁN, a saint's name, from Gaelic *ciar*, 'dark', and the diminutive ending -an. Other forms are Kieron, Kiaran.

Kira *see* CIARA

Kirsty (Scots, female)
An abbreviation of Christina but often now used on its own.

Kyle (Scots, male/female)
From Gaelic *caol*, 'strait'. An increasingly

popular name, perhaps in modern times seen as a masculine version of Kylie (*see also* GAEL) or Kayleigh (neither of which is Celtic in origin).

L

Labhra *see* LABRAID

Labraid (Irish Gaelic, male) *Lab-rad*
'Speaker'. This might indicate one who
speaks in assemblies, or a story-teller.
Labraid Loingseach, 'seafarer', 'shipman', is
a legendary leader and progenitor of the
men of Leinster. Other forms include
Labhraidh, Labhra, and it is anglicised into
Lowry.

Labraidh *see* LABRAID

Lachie *see* LACHLAN

Lachlan (Scottish Gaelic, male)
The name originally meant 'man from Scandinavia', Lochlann being the Gaelic for 'the land of fjords'. The pet form is Lachie.

Láeg (Irish Gaelic, male)
The name of Cuchulainn's charioteer and friend.

Lasair (Irish Gaelic, female)
'Flame, blaze'.

Laura *see* LOWRI

Leslie (Scots, male)
A location name from Aberdeenshire, from Gaelic *lios*, 'enclosure', and *liath*, 'grey'; often used as a personal name. This is the usual masculine form.

Lesley (Scots, female)
The usual feminine form of LESLIE.

Lewis (Scots, male)
Probably from French 'Louis', though it could be influenced by the name of the Isle of Lewis, which has been derived from Old Norse as *ljoth*, 'people', *hus* 'houses'. On the other hand, no other old personal names come from island names: Barra, for example, received its name from the personal name Barr, and not vice versa.

Lewis (Welsh, male)
A Welsh form of French Louis.

Liadain (Irish Gaelic, female) *Leea-dan*
Probably from Gaelic *liath*, 'grey'. The story of Liadain and her tragic love for the poet Cuírithir foreshadows the later one of Abelard and Héloise. Alternative forms are Líadan, Liadhain.

Liam (Irish Gaelic, male) *Lee-am*
Shortened from Uilliam, and the most usual Irish Gaelic form of William.

Lindsay (Scots, female/male)
From the surname Lindsay, which came to Scotland in the twelfth century, perhaps from Lindsey in England. An alternative form is Lyndsay.

Llew (Welsh, male) *Hloo*
From *lleu*, 'light', 'fair'. Lleu Llawgyffes, 'of the steady hand', son of ARIANRHOD, is a principal figure in one of the *Mabinogion* tales. The name may nowadays also be seen as a shortened form of Llywellyn.

Llian (Welsh, female)
'Flaxen'.

Llud (Welsh, male) *Hlood*
A legendary king of the ancient Britons. Anglicised as Lud.

Lloyd *See* LLWYD

Llwyd (Welsh, male) *Hloowid*
The Welsh root word means 'grey,' or 'holy',
a name for a priest.

Llywarch (Welsh, male)
Name of a sixth-century king. Llywarch Hen,
'the old', is the subject of an old Welsh poem,
'The Song of Llywarch the Old', lamenting
the ills of old age.

Llywelyn (Welsh, male) *Hloo-ell-in*
'Leader', from *llyw*, 'lead'. Llywelyn Fawr,
'the great', Prince of Wales, died in 1240. The
name is sometimes found spelt Llewellyn.

Loarn *see* LORN

Lonán (Irish Gaelic, male)
'Little blackbird'. From Gaelic *lon*, 'blackbird',
with the diminutive suffix -an.

Lorcan (Irish Gaelic, male)
'Fierce in battle', from *lorc*, 'fierce'. Anglicised

to Laurence, with which it has no etymological connection; hence the twelfth-century St 'Laurence' O'Toole should properly be St Lorcan.

Lorn (Scottish Gaelic, male)
From Loarn, one of the early rulers of the Dalriada Scots, one of the three sons of Erc, whose name is preserved in the Lorn district of Argyll. An alternative form is Lorne.

Lorna (Scots, female)
A feminine version of Lorn. The name was invented by the novelist R.D. Blackmore (1825–1900) for his novel *Lorna Doone* (1869).

Lorne *see* Lorn

Lowri (Welsh, female)
A Welsh form of Laura.

Lowry *see* Labraid

Lud *see* Llud

Lugaid (Irish Gaelic, male) *Loo-gad*
From Old Gaelic *lug*, 'light', a frequent warrior name in Old Irish sources, and going back
to the name of a major Celtic god, Lug.

Luned (Welsh, female)
Probably linked to Welsh *eilun*, 'idol', 'image'.
The heroine of a medieval Welsh legend,
Owain and Luned; daughter of the Lord of the
Fountain, she assists Owain to defeat him.
Also spelt as Eiluned. Other forms are Linet,
Lunet, Lynette.

Lyn (Welsh, male/female)
A diminutive of Llywelyn.

Lynette (Welsh, female)
See Luned. This name could also be a double
diminutive, with the French -ette suffix, 'little', ending added to Lyn.

M

Maadhbh *see* MEDB

Mab (Irish Gaelic, Welsh, female)
An abbreviated form of MEDB or Maeve. Not connected with Mabel, which is from Old French Amabel.

Mabon (Welsh, male)
This was the name of a Celtic god of youth, and maban is Welsh for 'child'.

Macbeth *see* BETHAN

Macha (Irish Gaelic, female) *Ma-ha*
The name of a goddess and legendary queen,

perhaps from Gaelic *magh*, 'plain', referring
to land.

Mackenzie (Scottish Gaelic, male/female)
Perhaps because of the Mackenzie River, this
surname, 'son of Kenneth', has become a
popular first name for girls in Canada.

Madoc *see* MADOG

Madog (Welsh, male)
Also spelt Madoc. From a Welsh root word,
maddeugar, indicating 'generous', 'forgiving'.
Madog was a renowned holy man of the seventh century. Madog ab Owain Gwynedd, a
twelfth-century Welsh prince, is reputed to
have sailed as far as America. His name is
preserved in that of Portmadoc.

Maebh *see* MEDB

Mael (Welsh, male) *Myle*
From Welsh *mael*, 'Prince'.

Maelgwyn (Welsh, male)
'Bright prince', from *mael*, 'prince', and *gwyn*, 'bright', 'fair'. Maelgwyn or Maelgwn Gwynedd was a king who lived during the sixth century.

Maeve *See* MEDB

Mai (Welsh, female)
The Welsh form of May.

Mailli (Cornish, Scottish Gaelic, female)
A form of Mary. The Scots form is Mallie.

Mair (Welsh, female)
The Welsh form of Mary.

Máire (Irish Gaelic, female) *Maur-ya*
Mary.

Máiread (Irish and Scottish Gaelic, female) *My-ratt*
Margaret.

177

Mairi (Scottish Gaelic, female) *Mah-ri*
Mary.

Mairin *see* MAUREEN

Máirtín (Scottish and Irish Gaelic, male)
A Gaelic form of Martin, after St Martin of
Tours, teacher of St Ninian, and who was
much esteemed by the Celts.

Mairwen (Welsh, female)
'Fair Mary', from *gwen*, 'bright'.

Maisie (Scots, female)
A pet form of either Marjory or Mary, also
found as a name in its own right.

Malachy (Irish Gaelic, male)
'Follower of St Seachlainn'. From Gaelic
maol, 'follower', 'disciple', and the personal name Seachlainn. It has also been
suggested the name can be interpreted as
'follower of Madog'. *See* MADOG. St

Malachy was in due course canonised himself. The name has a close resemblance to the Hebrew Malachi.

Malcolm (Scottish Gaelic, male)
'Servant of Columba', from Gaelic *maol*, 'servant', and Calluim, 'of Columba'. St Columba was venerated throughout Gaeldom, and this name was borne by four Scottish kings. Pet forms are Malc, Malkie.

Malise (Scottish Gaelic, male)
'Servant of Jesus', from Gaelic *maol*, 'servant', and *Iosa*, 'of Jesus'. This name is particularly associated with the Ruthven and Graham families.

Mallie *see* MAILLI

Malvina (English, female)
An invented Gaelic-sounding name from James Macpherson's eighteenth-century *Ossian* poems.

Manus (Irish Gaelic, male)
A Gaelic form of Magnus. Although a Latin name meaning 'great' it came to Gaeldom through the Norsemen, among whom it was a popular name.

Marcán (Irish Gaelic, male)
From Gaelic *marc*, 'steed'. A common name in early Irish literature, anglicised to Mark.

Mareddyd *see* MEREDUDD

Margaret *see* MÁIREAD, MARGED, MEGAN, PEGGY

Marged (Welsh, female)
Welsh diminutive form of Margaret. Also Margiad.

Margiad *see* MARGED

Mark *see* MARCÁN

(Welsh, male)
...adog'. From *mael*, 'follower'.

...saili (Scottish Gaelic, female) *Mar-sally*
A Gaelic form of 'Marjorie'.

Marvin see MERFYN

Mary see MAILLI, MAIR, MÁIRE, MAIRI, MAISIE, MAIRWEN, MÁIVE, MAUREEN, MELLE, see also GILMOUR

Massan (Scottish Gaelic, male)
The name of a saint, of uncertain origin; preserved in Glen Masan.

Maughold (Manx, male) *Maw-hald*
Name of a legendary Manx saint, who converted from being a pirate to the life of a holy hermit.

Maureen (Irish Gaelic, female)
'Little Mary'. Originally a diminutive, it has

long been a name in its own right. The Ga
form is Máirín.

Mavis (Scots, female)
'Singing bird'. In Scots the *mavis* is the song
thrush.

Mavourna *see* MAVOURNEEN

Mavourneen (Irish Gaelic, female)
'Darling little one', from Gaelic *mo*, 'my', and
mhuirnín, 'Little darling'. Originally and still
a term of endearment, it has also gone independent as a name. Another form is
Mavourna.

May (Irish and Scottish Gaelic, female)
Mai is Gaelic for the month of May; there is
also the Isle of May in the Firth of Forth.

Medb (Irish Gaelic, female) *Mave*
'Intoxicating', 'bewitching'. The name is probably cognate with Welsh *meddw*, 'drunk'. The

name of the legendary queen of Connaught who coveted the Brown Bull of Cooley. The legends invest her with magic powers and an intense attraction for men, few of whom however can stand up to her warlike nature. The source of the name is unclear. It has numerous forms including Madhbh, Maebh, and the anglicised (and most often used) form Maeve.

Medrawd (Welsh, male)
The bastard son of King ARTHUR, in the Round Table stories, anglicised as Mordred.

Megan (Welsh, female)
A Welsh diminutive of Margaret.

Melangell (Welsh, female)
'Honey angel'. The name of a saint, preserved in Llanfihangel.

Meilyr (Welsh, male)
'Man of iron'. Meilyr of Caerleon was a twelfth-

century wizard. Meilyr Brydydd (1100–1137) was chief bard to Gruffudd ap Cynan.

Meleri (Welsh, female)
This was the name of St David's grand-mother.

Melle (Breton, female)
The Breton form of Mary, it also has resonances in mel, 'honey'.

Merddyn *see* MYRRDIN

Meredith *see* MEREDUDD

Meredudd (Welsh, male)
'Great lord'. Also spelt Mareddyd. Maredydd ab Hywel Dda was a tenth-century king. An-glicised forms include Merideg, Meriadoc and, most commonly, Meredith.

Merfyn (Welsh, male)
Merfyn Frych was a ninth-century king of

Gwynedd. The source of the name has not been satisfactorily established. The anglicised form is Mervyn or Marvin.

Meriadoc, Merideg *see* MEREDUDD

Merlin, Merlyn *See* MYRDDIN

Mervin, Mervyn *See* MERFYN

Michael *see* MICHEÁL, MIHANGEL, MITCHELL

Micheál (Irish Gaelic) *Mee-hoyl*
The Gaelic form of Michael. A popular name in Ireland, with pet forms Mick, Mike, Mikey.

Midir (Irish Gaelic, male) *Mid-eer*
The name of a chief of the Tuatha Dé Danann, the lover of ETAÍN; portrayed as a proud and possessive figure.

Mihangel (Welsh, male)
The Welsh form of Michael.

Míl *see* MILES

Miles (Irish, male)
The normal origin of this name is from Latin
miles, 'soldier'; but its Irish link is with Míl,
also known as Míl Espáine, 'of Spain', last of
the legendary invader/settlers of Ireland, and
a source-point of numerous family
genealogies. An alternative form is Myles.

Mitchell (Scots, male)
A Scots form of Michael. The pet form is
Mitch.

Modwen (Welsh, female)
From *morwyn*, 'maiden'.

Moelwyn (Welsh, male)
'White, bare'.

Moina (Irish and Scottish Gaelic, female)
Perhaps stemming from *moine*, 'peat, moss':
girl of the peat-moss.

Moingionn *see* MONGFHIND

Moira (Irish, female)
An anglicised form of MAÍRE, though there is also a place and earldom of the same name in Ulster.

Mona[1] (Irish Gaelic, female)
Probably stemming from Gaelic *muadhnaid*, 'noble'.

Mona[2] (Welsh, Manx, female)
Mona was a name given by the Romans to a wide stretch of the West coast of Britain, and its islands. From it comes the Welsh name of Anglesey, Mon. But Man is also known as Mona's Isle.

Mongfhind (Irish Gaelic, female) *Mo-finn*
'Of the long fair hair', from Gaelic *mong*, 'long hair', and *fionn*, 'fair'. The name of numerous figures in history and legend, of whom the most prominent is the jealous step-mother

of NIALL of the Nine Hostages. Alternative forms are Mongfhionn, Moingionn.

Mongfhionn *see* MONGFHIND

Montgomery *see* MUIRCHERTACH

Mór (Irish Gaelic, female)
'Tall', 'big', from Gaelic *mór*. Itmay have been used as a subsitute for MÁIRE. Its diminutive form, Móirín, is often anglicised as MAUREEN.

Morag (Scottish Gaelic, female)
A Gaelic form of Sarah.

Moray *see* MURRAY

Mordred *see* MEDRAWD

Morfudd *see* MORWEN

Morgan (Irish Gaelic, Welsh, male/female)
Many powerful women have borne this

name, which traditionally originates with a Celtic war-goddess, still known as The Morrigan, from *mor*, 'great', and *gan*, which may mean either 'sea' or 'queen'. The name of Morgan Mwynfawr (seventh century) is preserved in Glamorgan. Although seen also as a boy's name, in the Arthurian romances Morgan le Fay is a witch queen.

Moriarty *see* MUIRCHERTACH

Morien (Welsh, male)
'Sea-born', from *mur*, 'sea'.

Morna *see* MUIRNE

Morven (Scottish Gaelic, female)
This name is probably related to MORWEN, though there is also the mountain Morven, from Gaelic *mór bhéinn*, 'big mountain'.

Morwen, Morwena (Cornish, Welsh, female)
'Maiden'. An older form is Morfudd; this was

the name of the woman loved by the bard DAFYDD ap Gwilym, unfortunately already married to someone else.

Muirchertach (Irish Gaelic, male) *Murr-hertah* 'Seafarer', from Old Gaelic *muir*, 'sea'. The name of a legendary high king, and frequently found in literature and records. It is anglicised into Moriarty and Montgomery (which properly has a non-Celtic etymology).

Muirne (Irish Gaelic, female) *Moor-na* The derivation is probably from Old Gaelic *muir*, 'sea', and means 'sea-bright' as in MURIEL. Muirne Muncháem, 'of the fair neck', was the mother of Fionn macCumhaill. There is a Gaelic diminutive form, Muirneag. Alternative forms are Muirenn, Muireann, Murna, Morna.

Mungo (Scottish Gaelic, male) This was a nickname of KENTIGERN, one of the great Celtic saints and patron of Glasgow Cathedral. Possibly from Old Welsh, *mwyn*, 'dear' and *cu*, 'amiable', meaning 'dear friend'.

Munro (Scottish Gaelic, male)
Surname of the Easter Ross clan, perhaps originally from Old Gaelic *mon ruadh*, 'red hill'.

Murchadh (Irish Gaelic, male) *Murr-hah*
Irish Gaelic form of MURDOCH, anglicised to Murrough, as is MURPHY.

Murdo *see* MURDOCH

Murdoch (Scottish Gaelic, male)
'Sea warrior', from Gaelic *murchaidh*, 'sea warrior'. The Gaelic form is MURCHADH. An alternative anglicised version is Murdo. Had the ambitions of the Albany Stewarts been gratified, Scotland might have had a king Murdoch instead of James I.

Muriel (Gaelic and Welsh, female)
'Sea bright', from Old Gaelic *murgheal*.

Murphy (Irish Gaelic, male)
A surname sometimes used as a first name
(and sometimes for a girl, especially in North
America). It derives from Gaelic *muir*, 'sea',
and *cú*, 'hound'. Other forms include
Murrough.

Murray (Scots, male)
From the surname Murray, a form of Moray,
from Old Gaelic *muir*, 'sea', and *ais*, 'edge, border'.

Murrough *see* MURCHADH, MURPHY

Myfanwy (Welsh, female) *Mih-van-wee*
'My fine one'.

Miles *see* MYLES

Myrddin (Welsh, male) *Mirr-thin*
The name appears to combine Old Welsh *myr*,
'sea', and *ddin*, 'hill'; it has been anglicised to
Merlin. The name of a celebrated wizard, first

recorded in the *Black Book of Carmarthen* (thir-teenth century), but going back to a sixth-cen-tury original. In the Arthurian legends he was made the tutor of King ARTHUR. His name is preserved in Carmarthen, 'fort of Myrddyn'. Alternative forms include Merlyn and Mervyn (but *see also* MERFYN).

N

Naísi *see* Naoise

Nancy *see* Agnes

Naoise (Irish Gaelic, male) *Nay-si*
The name of the eldest of the three sons of
Usna, and lover of Deirdre in the famous tale
from the *Ulster Cycle*. Also found as Naísi.

Naomh (Irish Gaelic, female) *Nayve*
From *naomh*, 'saint'. The use of this word as a
personal name is quite modern.

Neachtan, Nechtan *see* Nectan

Nectan (Pictish, male)
An ancient royal name; it was under their king Nectan that the Picts defeated the invading Anglians in AD 685. The name stems from a root-form *nig*, 'to wash', hence 'purified one'. The Pictish kings had a priestly role. Alternative forms are Nechtan, Neachtan.

Neil *See* NIALL

Nerys (Welsh, female)
'Lordly', from *Ner*, lord.

Nessa (Irish Gaelic, female)
'Ungentle'. The explanation lies in the traditional story of Nessa, mother of CONCHOBHAR, or Conor, macNessa. Originally called Assa, or 'gentle one', she was so fierce in defence of the kingdom of Ulster that her name was prefixed by *Ní*, 'not'.

Nest (Welsh, female)
Welsh form of Agnes. Also found as Nesta.

Nesta *see* NEST

Newlyn (Cornish, female)
The name of a Cornish town, its origin is cognate to Gaelic *naomh*, 'holy', and *linne*, 'pool'. Nuline is an alternative form.

Niall (Irish and Scottish Gaelic, male) *Nee-al*
'Champion'. From Old Gaelic *nia*, 'champion'. It was common for disputes to be decided by combat between rival champions from either side. Niall Noígiallach, 'of the Nine Hostages' was a celebrated fifth-century high king of Ireland, progenitor of the Ui Néill dynasty. Alternative forms include Neil, Neill, Neal, Neale. The English name Nigel has been associated with Niall, but the resemblance is coincidental.

Niam *see* NIAMH

Niamh (Irish Gaelic, female) *Nee-av*
'Radiant one'. Niamh of the golden hair,

daughter of the sea-god Manannan, fell in love with Oisin (Ossian), and took him to Tir nan Og. Alternative forms are Niam, Niav.

Niav *see* NIAMH

Ninian (Irish and Scottish Gaelic, male)
From the Old Gaelic personal name Ninidh, of uncertain derivation. St Ninian (fourth–fifth century) was one of the fathers of the Celtic Church in Scotland. The modern Gaelic form of the name is Ringean.

Ninidh *see* NINIAN

Nola *see* NUALA

Nominoë (Breton, male) *Nom-in-o-ay*
Name of a ninth-century Breton king who achieved Breton independence from the Frankish empire.

Norrie (Scots, male)
From the surname, stemming from Old Norse *norge*, 'Norway', indicating someone from that land. As a first name it may also be a pet form of Norman, although the ultimate source is very similar.

Norval (Scots, male)
A name invented by the eighteenth-century writer John Home in his play *Douglas*, though it has also been found as an old surname, a shortened form of Normanville, from the fourteenth century.

Nuala (Irish Gaelic, female) *Noola*
Probably an abbreviated form of FINNUALA. Nola is an alternative form.

Nudd (Welsh, male) *Nooth*
Name of a legendary Welsh hero, derived perhaps from the Brythonic god-name Nodons.

Nuline *see* NEWLYN

O

Oengus *See* ANGUS

Odhrán (Irish Gaelic, male) *Oh-rann*
From Gaelic *odhra*, 'dark-haired'. The name was borne by St Columba's associate and has strong connections with Iona. 'Reilig Odhrain' is the place where many kings and Lords of the Isles were buried.

Oisín *See* OSSIAN

Olave (Manx, male)
A Gaelic form of Norwegian Olaf, name of the founder of the Manx kingdom. This name is also used as a girl's name, prob-

ably as a variant of non-Celtic Olive or
Olivia.

Olwen (Welsh, female)
'White foot-print'. Name of the heroine of the
legend of 'Culhwych ac Olwen'.

Oonagh (Irish Gaelic, female) *Oo-na*
'The One'. A Gaelic form of Una, the maiden
rescued from the dragon in the legend of St
George.

Oran *See* ODHRAN

Orchil (Irish Gaelic, female)
A mythical name associated with an ancient
goddess of twilight.

Orfhlaith *see* ORLA

Orla (Irish Gaelic, female)
'Golden girl', from *ór*, 'gold'. Other forms are
Orlaith, Orfhlaith.

Orlaith *see* ORLA

Orna (Irish Gaelic, female)
'Dark-haired'. A feminine form of ODHRÁN.

Oscar (Irish Gaelic, male)
Perhaps from the root *os*, 'fawn', with the sense of 'deer lover'. In the later Fenian Cycle of legends, he is the son of Ossian, and a great poet and warrior.

Ossian (Irish and Scottish Gaelic, male)
Oisín, 'Little deer', from Gaelic *oisean*. Ossian, bard and warrior, son of FIONN macCumhaill, is one of the great figures of Gaelic legend, who, lured by NIAMH, spent hundreds of years in Tir nan Og, and emerged as young as he went in, only to age three hundred years and die in the space of a day.

Ottar *see* ARTHUR

Owan *see* OWAIN

Owain (Welsh, male)

A Welsh form of Eugenius, 'well-born', anglicised as Owen. A popular name in old Welsh legends, and the hero of the thirteenth-century poem 'Owain'. Owain Glyndwr was the last independent prince of Wales (*c.* 1350–*c.* 1416).

P

Paddy *see* PÁDRAIG

Pádraig (Irish and Scottish Gaelic, male) *Paw-rik*
'Of noble birth', a Gaelic version of Latin
Patricius, 'nobly-born'. Patrick is the anglicised
form. St Patrick (*fl.* fifth century) born to a
romanised British family on the West coast of
Britain, is the great missionary saint of Ireland,
and that country's patron saint. The name was
so popular in Ireland as for 'Paddy' and 'Irish-
man' to be synonymous to outsiders. The pet
forms Paddy and Patsy are usually found in
Ireland; Pat is more common in Scotland.

Pat, Patsy *see* PÁDRAIG

Patricia (English, female)
Not a Celtic name, but popular as the feminine form of Patrick (*see* PÁDRAIG).

Patrick *See* PÁDRAIG

Pawl (Welsh, male)
Welsh form of Paul.

Peadar (Irish and Scottish Gaelic, male)
Gaelic form of Peter.

Pedr (Welsh, male)
Welsh form of Peter.

Pegeen *see* PEGGY

Peggy (Irish, Scots, female)
Abbreviated forms of Margaret. In Ireland there is also the form Pegeen.

Peredur (Welsh, male)
The name of the hero of the Arthurian romance *Tair Rhamant*, a seventh son who undergoes magical adventures and may be either a precursor of, or derive from, Sir Perceval, knight of the Holy Grail in the English Arthurian tales.

Peronnik (Breton, male)
A Breton equivalent of Peredur.

Powel (Welsh, male)
'Son of Hywel', from *ap*, 'son'.

Proinséas (Irish Gaelic, male) *Phron-shas*
Gaelic version of Francis.

Pwll *see* Pwyll

Pwyll (Welsh, male) *Pull*
From *pwll*, 'wisdom', 'prudence'. Pwll, prince of Dyfed, is the hero of the first 'branch' of the *Mabinogion* tales.

R

Rab (Scots, male)
A pet form of Robert, occasionally found as a name in its own right. Another form is Rabbie.

Radha (Irish Gaelic, female) *Ra-ha*
'Far-seeing'. The name is related to Gaelic *radharc*, 'vision'.

Rae (Scots, male/female)
Originally a surname, perhaps from Gaelic rath, 'grace'.

Raghnailt (Irish and Scottish Gaelic, female) *Ran-ailt*
The feminine form of RAGHNALL.

Raghnall (Scottish Gaelic, male) *Ren-ull*
A Gaelic version of an Old Norse name brought by the Vikings, Rognvaldr, 'power in council'. It has numerous anglicised versions including Reginald, Ranald, Ronald, Randal.

Raibeart (Scottish Gaelic)
Gaelic form of Robert. *See* RAB.

Ranald See Raghnall

Regan (Irish Gaelic)
'King's consort', from *rí*, 'king', and *gan* 'queen'. The name gets a bad reputation in Shakespeare's *King Lear*.

Reginald *see* RAGHNALL

Reid (Scots, male)
A surname that is also found as a first name, from Scots *reed*, 'red'; also Gaelic *ruadh*, 'red'.

Rees *see* RHYS

Reynard *see* RHEINALLT

Rhedyn (Welsh, female)
'Fern'.

Rheinallt (Welsh, male)
A Welsh form of Reynard. Rheinallt was a fifteenth-century bard.

Rhian (Welsh, female)
'Fair maid', from *rhiain*, 'maiden'.

Rhiannon (Welsh, female)
'Fair maiden', but as the the name of a princess in the *Mabinogion* tales it also has the sense 'moon goddess' from the old British goddess Rigantona. An alternative form is Riannon.

Rhianwen (Welsh, female)
'Pure maiden'.

Rhisiart (Welsh, male)
Welsh form of Richard.

Rhodri (Welsh, male) *Rod-ree*
From a root form *rhod*, 'circle', 'disc', indicative of a crown or coronet. Rhodri Mawr, 'the great' was a ninth-century king of Gwynedd.

Rhona *see* RONA

Rhondda (Welsh, female)
'Slender', from *rhon*, 'lance', and by extension 'slim'. The name of a South Wales town in a narrow valley.

Rhonwen (Welsh, female)
'Fair and slender', from *rhon*, 'lance', and *gwen*, 'fair'.

Rhydderch (Welsh, male)
From *rhi*, 'king', dyrch, 'great', 'exalted'. The name of a famous king of Strathclyde in the sixth century; the ring found for him in a

salmon by St Mungo is incorporated in the arms of the city of Glasgow.

Rhydian (Welsh, male) *Ridd-eean. See* Rhydwen

Rhydwen (Welsh, male) *Ridd-wen*
'White, or blessed, ford'.

Rhys (Welsh, male) *Rees*
Rhys ap Gruffudd was a twelfth-century prince of Deheubarth (southern Wales). The anglicised form is Rees.

Riannon *see* Rhiannon

Rigantona *see* Rhiannon

Robat (Welsh, male)
Welsh form of Robert.

Robbie (Scots, male)
This pet form of Robert is now being used as a name in its own right.

Robyn (Welsh, male)
Welsh form of Robin. This spelling, outside
Wales at least, is often nowadays used as a
girl's name.

Roderick (Scots, male)
From Gaelic *ruadh*, 'red', and *rí*, 'king'; the
Gaelic form is Ruairidh. Cognate with Welsh
RHYDDERCH. Its pet forms include Rod,
Roddie, Rory.

Róisín (Irish Gaelic, female) *Rosh-een*
'Little rose'. As Róisin Dubh, 'Dark Rosaleen',
from a seventeenth-century Gaelic poem, the
name is synonymous with Ireland.

Rona (Scots, female)
Probably a feminine form of RONAN. There is
also the island of Rona, from Old Norse
hraun-ey, 'rough island', but as St Ronan lived
and died on North Rona, the two names are
intertwined. Also found as Rhona.

Ronald (Scots, male)
An anglicised version of RAGHNALL. Pet forms
are Ron, Ronnie.

Ronan (Scottish Gaelic, male)
'Little seal'. The likely derivation is Gaelic *ron*,
'seal', with the diminutive suffix -an. The
name of a famous Gaelic saint. *See also* RONA.

Ross (Scottish Gaelic, male)
From Old Gaelic *ros*, 'promontory', or 'wood',
and originally a surname, it is now widely
used as a first name.

Rowan (Scots, female/male) *Rau-an*
The name comes from the rowan tree, Gaelic
ruadhan, 'little red one', and is used both for
girls and boys. In the past rowan berries were
a specific against witchcraft, but the spread
of the name has been very recent.

Rowena (Welsh, female)
Perhaps an anglicised form of Welsh

Rhonwen. The name was used by Geoffrey of Monmouth in his *Historia Regum Britanniae* for the daughter of the fifth-century Saxon invader Hengist. The name was used by Sir Walter Scott for the heroine of *Ivanhoe*.

Roy (Scottish Gaelic, male)
From Gaelic *ruadh*, 'red'. A non-Celtic source of this name is from Old French *roy*, 'king'.

Ruairidh *See* RODERICK.

Ryan (Irish Gaelic, male)
Originally an Irish surname, from an Old Gaelic word meaning 'chief'. Nowadays it is an extremely popular first name in its own right, helped by the film star Ryan O'Neal.

S

Sadhbh (Irish Gaelic, female) *Sawv*
'Sweetness'. This was the name of the mother of Oisín, 'Ossian', who was turned into a deer.

Sanders (Scots, male)
A shortened form of Alexander.

Sandy (Scots, male)
A shortened form of Alexander. Once upon a time this name could be used, like Jock, as the synonym for a male Scot.

Saoirse (Irish Gaelic, female) *Sair-sha*
'Freedom'. Used as a personal name from the twentieth century, when Ireland regained its independence.

Sarah *see* MORAG

Saraid (Irish Gaelic, female) *Sarr-ad*
'Best one'. The name of the daughter of king *Conn* of the Hundred Battles, possessed of mystic skills.

Scáthach (Irish Gaelic, female) *Ska-hach*
The name of the warrior woman of the Isle of Skye who taught the arts of battle to CUCHULAINN and FERDIA. The source of the name is not clear, but it is not related to that of Skye itself, which comes from Old Norse. It is of historical interest in displaying close links between Alba and ERIN long before the emigration of the Scots.

Scota (Old Gaelic, female)
This name, whose derivation is not clear, is a generalised Latin name for an Irishwoman; but was borne as a personal name by two significant women of Gaelic legend, both said to be daughters of a pharaoh. The older Scota

is said to be the grandmother of Iber, founder of the Gaels; the younger was the second wife of Míl Espáine(*see* MILES).

Scott (Scots, male)
The surname of a Border clan, but a very popular and widely used first name for boys. It has, perhaps, been spread even further in the later twentieth century by Television's *Star Trek*. The pet form is Scotty or Scottie.

Scoular (Scots, male)
'Schoolmaster', literally 'schooler'. A South Scottish surname sometimes used as a first name.

Seachlainn *see* MALACHY

Sean (Irish Gaelic, male) *Shawn*.
An Irish Gaelic form of John. Alternative forms include Shaun, Shawn, Shane.

Seirian (Welsh, female) *Sye-reean*
'Bright one', a feminine form of SEIRIOL.

Seiriol (Welsh, male)
'Bright one', from Welsh *serennu*, 'sparkle'.
The name of a sixth-century saint, preserved
in the Welsh name of Priestholm island, Ynys
Seiriol.

Selwyn (Welsh, male)
A Welsh form of Julian. *See* SULIEN.

Sencha (Irish Gaelic, male) *Senn-ha*
'Historian'. The *seanachaidh* was the historian
and keeper of the traditions of the *tuath* or
clan.

Seóbhrach (Scottish Gaelic, female) *Sho-rach*
From the Gaelic *seóbhrach* meaning 'prim-
rose'.

Seonag (Scottish Gaelic, female) *Shon-ak*
Gaelic form of Joan.

Seonaid (Scottish Gaelic) *Sho-na*
A Scottish Gaelic form of Janet. The anglicised version Shona is often found. *See also* SINEAD.

Seóras (Scottish Gaelic, male)
A Gaelic form of George.

Seosamh (Irish and Scottish Gaelic, male) *Sho-sa*
The Gaelic form of Joseph.

Sétanta (Irish Gaelic, male)
The original name of CUCHULAINN.

Seumas (Irish Gaelic, male) *Shay-mas*
A Gaelic form of James.

Shannon (Irish, female)
The river name, perhaps related to Gaelic *sionn*, 'old', has found a new role as an increasingly popular name for girls, not inaptly as it had its own goddess, named Sinann or Sionan.

Sheila (Irish, Scots, female)
A version of Gaelic Sile, Celia. This name became highly popular in Australia, to the extent that all girls were 'Sheilas'. The version Shelagh is still found.

Shona *see* SEONAID

Sian (Welsh, female) *Shan*
Welsh form of Jane. Cognate with Gaelic SÍNE.

Siarl (Welsh, male) *Sharl*
Welsh form of Charles.

Siencyn (Welsh, male)
The Welsh form of English 'Jenkin', literally 'little John'.

Sile *see* SHEILA

Sileas (Scottish Gaelic, female) *Shee-luss*
Gaelic form of Julia.

Sím (Scottish Gaelic, male) *Sheem*
A Gaelic form of Simon, virtually a hereditary name among chiefs of Clan Fraser, who are known as MacSími.

Simwnt (Welsh, male)
The Welsh form of Simon.

Sinann *see* SHANNON

Sinclair (Scots, male)
From the Norman-French surname St-Clair, of a family who became earls of Caithness.

Síne (Irish Gaelic, female) *Sheena*
A Gaelic form of Jane or Jean. An anglicised form is found in Sheena and Sheana.

Sinead (Irish Gaelic, female) *Shin-aid*
Irish Gaelic form of Janet. Sinead Cusack, the actress, and Sinead O'Connor, the singer, have kept the name prominent.

Siobhán (Irish Gaelic, female) *Shiv-awn*
The Gaelic form of Joan, from Old French
Jehane. In the latter form it was introduced to
Ireland by the Normans in the twelfth century.
The actress Siobhán McKenna (1923–1986)
helped to establish the name in recent times.

Sion (Welsh, male)
The Welsh form of John. The diminutive is
Sionyn.

Sionan *see* SHANNON

Sior (Welsh, male)
The Welsh form of George.

Somerled (Old Norse, male), **Somhairlidh**
(Gaelic, male) *Sorr-lee*
The source of the name is Old Norse *sumar-
lioi*, 'summer warrior', referring to a Viking
raider. Its modern Gaelic form is Somhairle,
anglicised as Sorley and sometimes mistak-
enly as Samuel. Somerled, Lord of Argyll

(died 1164) was the ancestor of the Lords of the Isles. Sorley Maclean (1911–1996) was a great Gaelic poet of the twentieth century.

Somhairle *see* SOMERLED

Somhairlidh *see* SOMERLED

Sorcha (Irish and Scottish Gaelic, female) *Sorrha*
'Bright, radiant'.

Sorley *see* SOMERLED

Steffan (Welsh, male)
The Welsh form of Stephen.

Struan (Scottish Gaelic, male)
A territorial name from Perthshire, meaning in Gaelic *sruthan*, 'streams'. As a boy's name it is associated with the Clan Robertson, of the same locality.

Stewart (Scots, male)
Although the origin of the name is not Celtic, coming from Old English *stig-ward*, 'house-keeper', the name is wholly identified with Scotland through its adoption as a surname by the High Stewards of the kingdom. In the fourteenth century the Stewarts became the royal house. The French form Stuart has also been in use since the sixteenth century, and both forms are used as first names.

Stuart *see* STEWART

Sulien (Welsh, male)
'Sun-born'. This name is sometimes confused with Selwyn, 'Julian', and its Breton form Sulian.

T

Tadhg (Irish Gaelic, male) Taig
'Poet', 'bard'. A frequent name in Old Irish sources, and a tribute to the esteeem in which poets were held. Anglicised versions include Thady, Teague.

Taliesin (Welsh, male) *Tal-ee-sinn*.
'Radiant brow'. This was the name of one of the earliest of the great Old Welsh poets, said to have lived in the kingdom of Strathclyde in the sixth century.

Talorc, Talorg *see* TALORCAN

Talorcan (Pictish, male)
Name of a Pictish king who defeated the

Dalriada Scots in AD 736. Also recorded as Talorgan, and preserved in the place name Kiltarlity. Another form is Talorc or Talorg.

Tam (Scots, male)
A Scots abbreviation of Tammas, Thomas. A further pet form is Tammy, though this has also become a girls' name in its own right, from being an abbreviation of Tamsin.

Tara (Irish, female)
The anglicised form of Temair, name of the ancient capital of Ireland. It may mean 'mound' and be related to Gaelic *torr*, 'hill', 'tower'.

Tearlach (Scottish Gaelic, male) *Char-lach*
The Gaelic form of Charles, 'manly one', from Old German *carl*, 'man'.

Tegan *see* TEGWEN

Tegwen (Welsh, female)
'Beautiful, fair'. A feminine version of Tegyn,

name of an early Welsh saint. An alternative version is Tegan.

Tegyn *see* TEGWEN

Teilo (Welsh, male)
Name of a sixth-century saint, preserved in Llandeilo and many other places.

Teleri (Welsh, female)
From the River Tyleri in Monmouth.

Temair *see* TARA

Tewdwr (Welsh, male)
Anglicised as Tudor, a royal name long associated with Anglesey.

Thorketit *see* TORQUIL

Tierney (Irish Gaelic, female)
'Lordly', from Gaelic *tighearna*, 'lord'. *See also* TIGHERNAC.

Tighernac (Irish Gaelic, male) *Tyeer-nah*
'Lordly', from Gaelic *tighearna*, 'lord'. This
was the name of a celebrated annalist of
events in the Celtic world. An anglicised form
is Tierney.

Torcuil *see* Torquil

Tormod (Scottish Gaelic, male) *Torr-o-mot*
'Norseman'.

Tomos (Welsh, male)
Welsh form of 'Thomas'.

Torin (Scottish and Irish Gaelic, male)
Probably from a Norse name incorporating
that of Thor, god of thunder and war; 'thunder' in Gaelic is *torrunn*.

Torquil (Gaelic-Norse, male)
A name from Lewis in the Western Isles, from
Gaelic Torcuil, a form of Old Norse Thorketil,

'vessel of Thor'. Thor was the Norse god of thunder and warfare.

Treasa (Irish, female) *Tres-sa*
An Irish Gaelic form of Teresa, inspired particularly by St Teresa of Avila. Other forms of the name like Tracy, Tracey may come directly from Teresa rather than via the Gaelic form.

Trefor (Cornish, Welsh, male)
Originally a place name, from *tref*, 'settlement', and *vawr*, 'big', but long in use as a personal name. Anglicised as Trevor.

Trevor *see* TREFOR

Trina (Scots, Irish, female)
The latter part of CATRIONA, assuming an identity of its own as a girl's name.

Trystan (Cornish, Welsh, male)
This name has been linked to French triste, sad, but this is unlikely. The tragic romance

of the Cornish chief Trystan and Iseult of Ireland was drawn into the fabric of the Arthurian legends. Variants of the name include Tristan, Tristram.

Tudor *see* Tewdwr

Tyrone (Irish, male)
A territorial name, from the ancient kingdom Tir Eógain, 'land of Eogan', still a county in Ireland, made popular as a first name in the twentieth century by the film star Tyrone Power and the drama producer Tyrone Guthrie.

U

Ughes *see* UISDEAN

Uilleam (Scottish Gaelic, male) *Eel-yam*
The Scottish Gaelic form of William. The name, from Old German, means 'strong helmet'. *See* LIAM.

Uilliam *see* LIAM

Uisdean (Scottish Gaelic, male) *Oosh-tyan*
A Gaelic form of Ugues, Norman-French HUGH. The meaning of the name is 'spiritual one'.

Una *See* OONAGH

Urien (Welsh, male)
Name of a fifth-century king of the land of
Rheged, in what is now southern Scotland.
He was incorporated into the Arthurian leg-
ends, sometimes as the husband of the witch-
queen MORGAN le Fay.

Uther (Welsh, male)
From *uthr*, 'terrible'. Uther Pendragon, 'head
leader', was the second husband of IGRAINE
and the father of King ARTHUR.

V

Valda (Cornish, female)
'Flower', from a Cornish word cognate with Welsh *blodyn*, 'flower'.

Valmai (Cornish, Welsh, female)
Perhaps 'mayflower', from *blodyn*, 'flower', and mai, 'May'.

Veryan *See* BURYAN

Vivian (English, female)
Not a Celtic name, but has often been assumed to be one through the supposition that it is an anglicised form of Béibhinn.

W

Wallace (Scots, male)
The name is cognate with 'Welsh', and means an inhabitant of the originally-Brythonic kingdom of Strathclyde, which existed up to the end of the tenth century. The surname of the great defender of Scotland's liberty in the thirteenth/fourteenth century Wars of Independence, William Wallace, it became a popular surname in the twentieth century. Another form is Wallas.

Wallas *see* WALLACE

Watkin *see* GWATCYN

Wendy (English, female)
Of interest because it is one of the few invented names to become popular. It was first used by the Scottish writer J.M. Barrie in Peter Pan (1904), and gained popularity quite quickly.

William *see* LIAM, GWILYM, UILLEAM

Wyn (Welsh, male)
From *gwyn*, 'white, pure'.